Dear Teacher, You're Enough

Finding the Needed Grace, Compassion, and Patience to Carry On

by
Christina Lindvay

©2024 by Christina Lindvay

Published by hope*books
2217 Matthews Township Pkwy
Suite D302
Matthews, NC 28105
www.hopebooks.com

hope*books is a division of hope*media

Printed in the United States of America

First paperback edition.

Paperback ISBN: 979-8-89185-204-4
Hardcover ISBN: 979-8-89185-205-1
Ebook ISBN: 979-8-89185-121-4
Library of Congress Number: 2024945966

hope✳books
hopebooks.com
Because the world needs your hope-filled
words now more than ever

"*Dear Teacher, You're Enough* is an encouraging, friendly, inspiring, and down-to-earth resource so needed for us educators right now. With grace, openness, and vulnerability, Christina Lindvay transforms into words her own personal, lived experiences of being in the classroom—both as an educator and mother—during these fragile and uncertain times.

Lindvay writes, "As teachers, we're taught the relationship we have with our students is paramount, the relationship we have with their families is crucial, but no word is mentioned about the relationship we have with ourselves. It is the foundation for it all." With compassion and patience, Lindvay models how we *can* come to know our own unique inner voice—untangled from the internalized pressures and demands teaching has on us—and that this knowing can paradoxically bring us into a more real and grounded sense of our shared "teacherhood."

From societal injustices to the health of our fingernails, *Dear Teacher, You're Enough* gently invites us teachers—at any page in the book—to arrive alongside and settle into the gift of our own ever-growing, already complete, human fullness—exactly as we are."

–**Kristin**, Teacher, California

"Christina is a natural teacher. I saw it with my own eyes."

–**Carrie LaFuria**, Teacher, Pennsylvania

"*Dear Teacher, You're Enough* is an essential read for every educator who has ever questioned their worth or struggled to carry the weight of the classroom. Christina Lindvay's words are a lifeline, reminding us that grace, compassion, and patience aren't just for our students—they are gifts we must offer ourselves. Her deeply personal reflections, combined with practical wisdom, create a guide that is as nurturing as it is transformative. If you've ever felt the strain of teaching or wondered if you're truly making a difference, this book will remind you that you are enough, just as you are."

–Lisa Baylis. M.Ed
author of "Self-Compassion for Educators"

Dedication

This book is dedicated to the teachers of Erie and Oakland.
You are impactful beyond measure.
May you always remember this.

&

To my family, always.

When They Ask, I'll Say

Teachers are tired
and they need love
they need to know they're enough
Not perfect but enough

Stay in the game
You are building rewards

You
are
the
conduit
Between this generation and the next

So keep
on going
I promise
you'll be OK

You are enough
I love you

–Christina Lindvay

Contents

INTRODUCTION

A Letter to You

Dear Teacher,

I am like you. A highly qualified educator who's reached their limit. Who understands that teachers are human beings who need the same love and care that we give to our students. We give so much to others, and we must extend it to ourselves, too. I believe this is one way we can make this *work*, work for us.

In spite of all that has happened—and *is still happening*—you still have a sparkle to you. I know this, and my mission is to help you see this, too. It's taken me a long time to see who I am beyond my experiences, my hardships, and who I am when I fail in the roles I hold so dearly.

It's that very struggle I want to help you with. It's what I've been called to do. Called to you. It is not a surprise to me our paths have crossed. Out of the billions of words you could have read today, you came to these. After all, they were written for you.

For you, the teacher who:

- Holds more than you can carry.
- Excels, but still feels full of doubt.

- Questions which path is the right to take when there are so many options.
- Experiences joy, but is at a loss when it flees.
- Feels like a failure when mistakes are had.
- Desperately wants to be on the side of "good" and "right" and "true."
- Is unsure why you can't meet your goals.
- Is confused why your goals keep changing.

And, who strives more than you sing.

You care so deeply and want to succeed. And the road has been challenging. It's been bumpy and downright painful. You so badly want to make a difference, but somewhere along the way, your perfectionist tendencies got the better of you. *Life* got the better of you.

Maybe you've forgotten how much you've achieved. Or become hyper-focused on all you have yet to do. Or lamented that you'll never be able to achieve your dreams.

Something got in the way.

Someone got in the way.

And even when you've been able to see or move a little past your internal struggles, you've been slammed with the overwhelm of modern-day teaching. Seeing the profession you love so profoundly become a literal battleground is maddening. It's frustrating to watch you and your colleagues know a better way forward yet feel silenced by school and state administrations. And you simply cannot take another overcrowded classroom with little to no emotional support.

I know all of this because I've been there. I got my start in day-to-day substitute teaching and then landed a fourth-grade placement. I spent the next ten years teaching Kindergarten in classrooms from Pennsylvania to California. From Traditional to Montessori, I've seen the ins and outs of public, private, and charter school classrooms, as well as serving on the Executive Board as President of a Preschool. My last teaching placement was as a part-time Reading Support Specialist while tending to my then-one-year-old-twins.

At that time, I felt like life was opening up for me. My family was planning a move to Canada, and I couldn't wait for my next step in education to take off. However, as much as I loved that last placement, it was also the one that threw a wrench in my philosophy. It completely changed the way I saw education.

And then, my internal upheaval led to grief as I came face-to-face with dreams of mine that were broken. What was about to be the start of a great career switch into helping teachers with their mental health instead turned into a five-year, 'What am I even doing with my life?' tailspin. Day to day, it looked more like reaching, slipping, falling, grasping, striving, failing, failing, getting back up, getting spit back out, CHURN, CYCLE, and REPEAT.

At this time, external factors took hold, too. A global pandemic occurred, and there was a resurgence of the Civil Rights movement. We were thrown, once again, into the muddy waters of a Presidential election, and we watched, stunned and angered, as more schoolchildren and adults died from gun violence. Amid it all, legislation changes have left more questions than answers, more fears than hope. We are in wars we're only beginning to name.

Did I miss anything?

We do not live in a vacuum. What is outside comes in. And what's inside goes out. And that's where we're going to focus.

Throughout the book, sometimes I'll be speaking to you, the collective you—*us*—because we are part of the larger organization of educators. We share struggles and triumphs and are all too familiar with what happens when under-resourced. We all understand what it's like to be in the modern classroom. And we know that any one issue transcends us as individuals. Sometimes, speaking to the crowd is what's needed. Sometimes, knowing that others are in this with us can make us feel less alone. And I know how much it is needed right now. We are stronger together.

Other times, I'll be speaking to you, the individual, the person holding this text in their very hands right now. I know you are the soul on the other side. So often, as readers, we need to know the author is looking out for us. *I am.* We need validation that they understand the challenges we face. *I do.* And we need reassurance that they can guide us to somewhere new. *I will.* I see you, friend.

I share my classroom experiences and stay-at-home experiences because they have served as the backbone of this work. During the years I've wrestled with my job title, the most challenging thing is invalidating myself because of my struggles. I've felt the sting of not meeting my own expectations. *Am I more of a teacher? Am I more of a parent? How can I be a teacher's teacher if I am a parent who cannot keep it together? Clearly, I am in no form to try and help others do the same.* But now, on this side of it, it feels inadequate to relegate my teaching experiences to only those in the classroom when some of my greatest lessons have come from outside of it. They are what brought me to you.

I'm here because I get you. I've had years in the mud and ones that felt like I was soaring. I'm well-educated and well-trained, but I still suffer from doubt and worry attacks. I've been dragged, almost quite literally, by the demands of children, adults, and parents. I've wanted to walk completely away from education. I suppose in some ways I have. I did.

But I am back. Because I missed you. I missed me. I missed what we are. And because I know who we are, I can't walk away again.

There are struggles I've faced internally and struggles I've faced externally. There are things I've learned on the inside and things I've learned on the outside. Teachers like us who have a loud inner critic need to discover ways to quiet that demanding voice so we can do the work that matters to us. We need to learn ways we can replace our perfectionism for power. We do not need to get rid of this, which strengthens us, but we do need to move it around occasionally. That's what we're going to focus on throughout this book.

By exploring common thoughts I've had, I'll move us through my experiences in and out of the classroom so that you can better see yourself. My greatest hope for this book is that you feel *seen and heard*, to borrow a phrase from maternal mental health advocate and illustrator Jamina Bone. In fact, it's through her graciousness and others like her—including professional help—that I have come to know the grace, patience, and self-compassion needed to do this work. The means are the end. These means matter.

Unfortunately, we will not be able to fix education alone. But there are things we can do to stand in our power. Whether it's an inside or an outside pressure, we can still take action, even if that action sometimes means resting—especially in uncertain times, especially when life throws curve balls. Especially as human beings with a feeling heart, we need ways to move forward when life gets hard. Because life *will* get hard.

As we move through the chapters, I'll help you find ways to offer yourself grace and love—the very things you show to students and their families every day. I'll offer you resources and suggestions for ways you can empower your own journey and find strength starting today. We don't have to be our own worst enemy anymore.

In the safe space of this book, I will hold you. I will help you. Together, we may even heal a little bit more than we thought was possible.

While I'm not a licensed therapist or counselor, I will guide you through tools, strategies, and tips to help you see what's never been yours to carry. I will help you lighten your load—so that even if your day-to-day responsibilities do not change, you will be afforded new ways to carry on. You will begin to move about your days with more lightness and ease because you will no longer carry the weight of the world on your back. You will begin to see, just as I have, how becoming aware of the internal and external pressures we face can bolster us to establish better boundaries. It can help us see what is and isn't our responsibility. Life can take us out for the count, but we can put ourselves back together with the right tools. We get to be the observer and the chooser. Together, we get to create the field of Education we wish to see.

These stories, snippets, and reminders of my hard times can serve as a light in the dark. If you can't see anything else right now, see this. See me. So you can see yourself. I'm here for your good days and also your bad. I'm here because I want to be here. For it. For all of you.

I'm not here to congratulate you on those stellar lesson days (which I will still be doing because you absolutely deserve it). I'm writing this at 4:52 am because I also understand the days that immobilize you. That make you not want to get out of bed. Or, in my case, today, the days you get up hours before your alarm because anxiety is gnawing at your toes. I'm here for the days that consume you with so much worry that you don't want to share any of your struggles. Maybe you can't share your struggles. Perhaps it may pose too much risk, and you don't have the emotional safety to release. I'm aware of that, too. Teacher, that's why I am here.

This book was born at the intersection of love, belonging, purpose, and connection. All the roads led me to you. If this is beginning to sound a bit like a love letter, GOOD; that is exactly its intention.

Although I can't possibly know your situation exactly or the exact history you bring to your work, there are a few inconsequential things I'm willing to bet: you probably have a teacher bag, you may or may not be reading this in your bed on a school night, now that I made you aware of that, you're realizing you should probably go to sleep (but just, like, a couple more pages, right?). By the way, what kind of tea are you drinking?

Hi. Okay, I'm not trying to be *all* up in your business. But friend, talk to me. Let me talk to you. *With* you. That's why I am here. I see you whether you've been in the classroom for one, ten, or an astounding twenty years.

I absolutely understand the pressures we face. And maybe, just maybe, I understand the pressure you put on yourself to perform. To be perfect. To have to know it all and do well. With no mistakes. To tell kids that trying your best and making mistakes is part of learning, except when it comes to you who wants to get it right the first time. (For my more experienced teachers here, perhaps you can chuckle to yourself that you ever thought that was the way forward).

We are losing good teachers to strain and doubt. This book is a walk in self-care, self-compassion, and growing grace for who we are and what we can do. You'll have opportunities to reflect on your life to see where *patience* might meet your *hard*. Together, we'll build the resilience needed to keep going. We may even get to change Education along the way.

As much as I would like to, I won't have all the answers for you, but I'll be with you while you find them. I am a guide by your side, so you don't have to go through the hard alone. I will show you how I persevered through some of my biggest struggles in and out of the classroom and how I truly believe you can do the same without jeopardizing your values, morals, and priorities. In fact, reading this book may help you reexamine what's most important to you.

Maybe we won't always hit the mark, and that's OK, because you're still showing up for yourself, and that's really what this work is about. So, come. Let's do this together. You are enough, and you've always been enough.

Two of the most persistent thoughts I've had as an overwhelmed high-striver are, "I can't do this anymore," followed by, "But I should know better." Together, they left me feeling inadequate and ashamed. Then, doubt would join the party, and soon, I was sipping a triple-infused concoction that left me dazed. I was unable to do the work that mattered to me. This fed the cycle even more.

I knew I needed another way. I trust you're seeking one, too.

For this, I've divided the book into two parts. Part One follows the theme of "I Can't Do This Anymore." We'll delve into stories, situations, and experiences—both in and out of the classroom—that relate to moments of being at our limit and not feeling good enough. We'll look at what's behind many of these feelings and unpack how our past informs our present. This leads us to Part Two, "I Need a New Way." I offer you numerous tools and frameworks that have immensely helped me live with more ease. These are what have made my life as a teacher—and my life outside of teaching—more sustainable.

Starting in Chapter One, "You're a Good Teacher," I lay out two paths you can take to help you see your challenges in a new light. To lead you to a life with more self-compassion, grace, and patience so you can carry on even through rough terrain. The bumps may not fully go away (we'll learn that's not the point). Therefore, I provide guide rails for emotional support. Sometimes, that's learning to tell ourselves new words.

The chapter titles themselves also tell a story, and each chapter starts with an affirmation, mantra, or "look-out" for what's to come. Additionally, each one ends with an invitation to pause and consider how you can apply the content. Will you take a shortcut or the scenic route? That's up to you. (That's a bit of a trick question—both are entirely acceptable at different times. You'll learn that, too.)

As you enter the following pages, notice what comes up for you along the way. Jot down what doesn't jive. Highlight what does. Create your own headings and questions, and, by all means, write in the margins! Sometimes, we don't realize we need permission to do a thing, so let this be yours. This is your space. You can rest here.

And, dear teacher, it's OK to pause. To breathe. To take the time you need. There is no rush. In fact, you'll also find *Space for You* at the end of this book, pages you are free to use as you wish. Come back as often as needed.

Love, in the truest and most noble way possible,

Christina

Let's begin!

PART 1

I Can't Do This Anymore

1

You're a Good Teacher

I am peace.

Undoubtedly, it's been hard. It's been so very hard. But, if I may, it's also been good. Like, really, really good. And I think you know this, too. And that's where we're going to start.

I know that for as many hard days (or years) as you've had, you've also had good ones. Great ones. Stellar ones. Shanna Schwartz from the Teacher's College at Columbia University dubbed these her "Beyoncé Days." These are days that every imaginable thing goes right or as close to right as one can expect. These are the days you feel at the top. You *are* at the top.

The stars aligned just for you.

You woke up early, ate breakfast, and got off to school, carrying the excitement of a lesson you're about to try. You feel rested and rejuvenated to take on this next day. When you get out of your car, you're excited to take the next step. You're even excited to see that one student who's always early. You may even give a genuine hello to a coworker. Your school doesn't smell but instead reminds you of home. You feel at home. Ease washes over your body.

You switch on the lights in your classroom, awash with pride. You created this. You and your class community. So much good happens here. So much hard work. And you get to witness it all.

You glance at the clock as you write the morning message on the board. Wow, you still have 20 minutes to prepare! Gold! You lay out the necessary materials to start your morning and feel secure knowing that your head is screwed on tightly today.

When the bell rings, you take a necessary breath, and a smile widens across your face. Maybe it's a little forced out of habit, but there's more truth in it today.

As your morning work period is underway, you notice how much calmer you are. It hasn't been a perfect morning; you've already had to redirect children 20 times, but you have had the capacity to handle it. *Yes, you are a good teacher*, you think. This thought fills you with relief, joy, and gratitude. You're not the sum of your hard days. Today's proof of that.

Morning turns to late morning, and you're still feeling like gold. You're loving the body you're in. You're feeling it, too. The outfit you chose—priceless. Today's internal dialogue has been: If you look good, you feel good; if you feel good, you skate good. And you feel great.

Better than great, you feel on fire. Maybe you're a bit more Alicia Keys than Beyoncé. During independent workshop time, you usually can conference and work with about three children before volcanoes erupt. On average, you may be able to meet with one small group, but today? Oh, today's been a gold mine! You got to conference with five children individually. You met with one small group on the carpet. You also gave an entire table a quick coaching moment. You redirected 15 more times, but it worked 15 times. Things are moving.

You're coaching and connecting. Connecting and coaching. This is what it feels like to be a good teacher.

The day ends, and you're tired, but you're not exhausted. You're sleepy but not spent. You may have even had some meaningful conversations with parents, the kind you walk away from feeling seen and appreciated.

What a good day!

Takeout tonight, baby!

Does that sound something like it? Maybe not detail for detail, but somewhere between here and there. Perhaps not these past few years, but the ones before it? Yeah? Those days remind you how awesome you are. You *are* a good teacher. That thought permeates your being.

Let's take the memory and the feeling of your glorious days and carry it into right now. Let it fill you with what you need to move forward peacefully and consciously. What do those days look like for you? Close your eyes or jot it down now.

You've had good days. You've had amazing days. These moments of calm, softness, ease, and joy make you want to melt. And they make you want to scream! That's what makes the hard feel harder. You know you deserve so much more. The back and forth, the yo-yo, is tiring. It's exhausting. Why things work one day and not the next is frustrating. It all feels like a contradiction. *I thought I just said I was a good teacher?*

I hope you learn throughout this book that there is solace in that, too. It doesn't make you a good teacher on some days and a bad teacher on others. You are worth all of the good. The good never leaves. The fact you're here makes you a "good" teacher. You care so deeply.

I could write a whole book about the generosity and brilliance of Brené Brown. She's shared so much research and guidance on better holding our vulnerability and reaching for courage. I learned of its surprising payoff one time during my first year teaching.

In the middle of a lesson with my fourth-graders, who wanted absolutely nothing to do with what I was saying, I excused myself to go cry in the bathroom (on my birthday, no less!). As I looked into the mirror and saw my blotchy-red face, shame and fear took hold. *I can't return like this, everyone will know!* I willed the clock to freeze. Out of options, I wet a paper towel with cool water and pressed it on my cheeks. I gently swiped my ring finger from one corner of my eye to the other. I took one last deep breath and then opened the door. I gasped. My colleague stared back at me. *"This is it. I'm a goner. There goes my credibility,"* I thought. Instead, one look was all it took, and she knew what had happened. She gave me a hug, a pep talk, and an invitation to hang out later that evening. With each step back to my classroom, shame dissolved, and courage formed.

Showing vulnerability and courage aren't always easy things to do, but in doing so, we develop our character and trust that we will come out stronger and more connected on the other side.

If I hadn't let myself cry, would I have realized I could be supported in my tough moments? Would I have shown myself I can have a trying encounter and still return to face others?

While teaching is one of the most painfully giving professions, where we witness many lows, it also uplifts. It can give us the best feeling in the world. As Brené Brown's research on vulnerability goes, however, you can't have one without the other. You can't bypass the undesirable "bad" feelings and only expect to see the "good" ones.

I put those in quotations to highlight that it's often our common misconception and learned belief that feelings are one way or another rather than being neutral. This will be important to remember as we move forward. For now, it's enough to recognize that the differences or extremes of these states create a balance. And the more deeply you're willing to go to one side, the more likely you are to reach the extreme of the other. When we can be honest about our vulnerabilities and grief, we can also experience the highs of connection and joy. In short, our "bad" days also give us more Beyoncé! Yay!

As we examine and dive deeper into these flux states, you'll also notice the theme of *impermanence* woven throughout the chapters. Impermanence is defined as the state of lasting for only a limited time.[1] Good and then bad. Bad and then good. This concept floored me when I first heard about it. How much had I been suffering, believing everything was always supposed to be good?! It never occurred to me that things—life—will also be hard.

While it is helpful to know about impermanence in the tough moments because it reminds us that this is not a forever state, I recognize it is also frustrating. Depressing, perhaps. We want the good all of the time! Give us more Beyoncé! But I weave it throughout the book because it allows us to see *what is* versus what we *expect* life should be. It does not condone the unjust and wrong or make the frenzied days when you woke up late, got a flat tire, forgot to bring in materials, or had an unpleasant conversation with a parent any easier, but it does create space for us to see our humanity. It also lets us see we cannot live alone on a high. Sorry, not Beyoncé all of the time.

We realize we're not alone in our suffering when we see our shared humanity. It's my goal for you to see you're not alone right now. And I hope you will begin to see your hard days as just that, hard. They're not hard because you're a terrible teacher or lacking. They're hard because we're up against so much. There is much out of our control. We will look at exactly what those barriers are in the upcoming chapters.

While there are things we can do to become grounded and aware of our circumstances, you must understand that where you come up short in the classroom does not have to do with lack. You are already highly qualified. There isn't "one more thing" for you to learn. Unfortunately, you will not become a gold-medal teacher by reading these words. At the risk of making you close this book for good, I daresay you don't even need them. You already have all that you need. (But, maybe, keep going and make that decision later.)

Our hard days become a practice that helps us see that we are humans carrying a heavy load. Unfortunately, in the classroom, the odds have often been stacked against us.

Even so, I know that as hard as it's been, you're not done yet. Ok, maybe one foot's been out the door! But I believe your heart's still in it, even if it's tiny pieces. You can still show up, fight, and recognize your power and wholeness. Because you are a good teacher. And it's time you see that, too. I will show you how to do that by befriending your humanity, building your courage, and strengthening your self-compassion. *Grace* and *Patience* will become new friends.

I understand you won't always be able to hold this presence. I can't either. We can't force positivity when our bodies beckon us to slow down and recognize the grief we've been up against: the hurt, the pain, the shame. It knows what game you've been playing.

But your body is also asking you to be on your team. For you to be both coach and player, depending on your needs. To borrow the words of anti-bias, anti-racist educator and speaker

Britt Hawthorne, "Your life is *rooting for you*."[2] It's waiting for you to plant yourself in your wildest dreams. Life doesn't have to be a miracle, a fantasy, or a forlorn mirage. It can happen right now.

Believe me, there is much I wish to change about education. That would require a whole volume of books. But for this one, when it comes down to it, I want us to have each other's back and drop the facade that we're doing OK when we're not. I want our vulnerability to shine through as much as I want our joy to pop. I want us to recognize ourselves in another and be able to walk this road together, not alone. We don't need to feel alone when surrounded by so many people (though I know that we have). But in order to connect, we have to drop self-sabotaging behaviors, such as:

> Perfecting
> Presenting
> Competing
> Ignoring
> Judging
> And gossiping.

Instead, we need to pull up the bar on:

> Loving Kindness
> Connection
> Realness
> Truth
> Beauty
> And, of course, honoring our hell or high water Beyoncé days.

More than anything, I want you to see that you are allowed to make mistakes. The world won't fall apart if you stop. You don't have to hustle for your worth. And you can still make changes. But you need to be aware of what's been getting in the way, and I will help you see this and recapture who you are. *You are not alone.*

This is the way forward, and it's the kind of system I want to belong to. I want to be unafraid of being human. I want to be a teacher who excels and is fearless in failing. Who recognizes her faults and limits and doesn't use them as excuses but invites grace and compassion into the crevices. We must notice our brain activity, or it will own us—this is not a judgment but a fact.

So, how do we do that? How might we use the memory of our Beyoncé days and examine our inner thoughts to recognize the power we have inside of us right now? How might we look at the external pressures surrounding us to realize that we've been carrying more than we should?

We take a new path.

I have two to share with you. Both will take us to the *Land of And.* Doesn't that sound magical already? Grab your teacher bag, and let's go.

The first path is a quick and continual one. Truthfully, both paths are continuous. We will cycle through them as needed. But the first path is unique because you can use it anytime you're experiencing tension. When you're noticing those flustered feelings emerge. When you're unsure why that kid is behaving the way they are. And you find yourself on the brink of making a choice out of habit rather than response. The first path is there with you. It's the I-Need-Something-Right-Now Path, and we can remember it with its acronym: PATH.

Pause
Ask Yourself What's Really Going On
Think About What You Need
Hold Your Humanity

This first path allows us to notice tension and mindfully respond. It puts a pause before our reaction. It makes room for necessary breaths. It's always available to you.

The second path is the *Keep Calm And* Path. We're all familiar with "Keep Calm and Carry On," but this path goes further. It goes beyond. We go under the surface and really meet ourselves. Doing this frees us.

The *Keep Calm And* path is the cycle and nature of this work of building courage and befriending our humanity. Inherently, it reminds us there's so much more we need to care for our wellbeing properly. Rather than keep calm and carry on, I offer the following:

Keep Calm *AND*

>*Cry a Little or A Lot*
>*Name Your Feelings*
>*Name Your Grief*
>*Give Yourself Grace and Self-Compassion*
>*Remind Yourself You're Not Alone*
>*And That You Can Do This, so*
>*Dust Off the Cheeto Powder*
>*Do the Next Thing*
>*And then, and only then,*

Carry On.

The chapters in this book do not follow this path with a one-to-one correspondence, but the overall trajectory of my story and offerings honors these steps. This process is rarely linear. If it feels easier, you can turn this path into a circle or even a roundabout. Get off when you need to, or circle as many times as necessary.

Both paths meet you where you are and walk with you to your next step. They remind us we're divinely human with flaws and feats. And they also take you to the *Land of And*.

A few years ago, when I started using Instagram and social media in a new way to find inspiration and motivation, I came across an image of a garden. It was a mix of greenery and wildflowers, calm and inviting. At the top, it read, "Stop pulling up your roots," and then at the bottom, "Growth doesn't happen in a day." I've come across different versions of that over the years since, and each time, I'm reminded of *patience*.

Progress takes time. We educators understand that. We recognize that it can, and should, often take a whole school year to see the hard work begin to flower, but when it comes to ourselves, well, that advice is better given to others.

As a teacher, you give your students the benefit of time. You understand their development and that only some things will come to them in one day. You know that they are going to make mistakes before they show growth. Moreover, you understand that their mistakes are *part of* their growth. But when it comes to yourself, how often do you disregard your own progress? How often do we bemoan we're not seeing results fast enough? How likely are we to dig out the seeds before we sprout? Uproot the plant before we bloom?

You can't see me, but I am raising my hand. I know this feeling very well. I've experienced it time and time again.

It can feel achingly painful to be in the waiting.

In the crossing

On the bridge

In dreaded limbo

But with new eyes and going through this process, it's also the *Land of And*.

In this land:

You can love teaching **and** hate parts of it. You can strive every day for your students **and** still come up short. You may only reach some of your students in a day **and** that's still a win. You can't do it all **and** this doesn't make you a bad teacher. You don't have to do this work perfectly **and** that still makes you a good teacher.

And, perhaps, most close to my heart: You can make mistakes with children **and** still know what's best for them. Your inability to do it perfectly does not invalidate you, your knowledge, or your heart. You are still worthy. Echoing the ethos of artist and creator Jamina Bone, *You are still a good teacher.*[3]

You get to be free. Because you get to be both. And both is where I want to live. Holding "both" allows us to be human AND on our way. *Both* gives us the freedom to own our mistakes AND understand they don't define us. *Both* is the "PASS GO" of the 21st century.

"When do I collect my $200?" you may be asking.

There's so much I wish I could tell new-teacher-me. While so much of my life was viewed in a binary, now I see that we truly live in the *Land of And*. This and that. Good and bad. Both can exist. Often at the same time! Sometimes, these experiences will feel contradictory, but operating from a place where we welcome this nuance allows us to live with more self-compassion, grace, and patience. For who we are and who we're becoming. I didn't always know this land, but now that I do, I don't want to leave it. And, it's here, ready for you to inhabit it, too.

I start this book with the good days because they matter. They sustain us, remind us why we do this work, and, paradoxically, help us better see our difficult days.

As mentioned before, I want to clarify that when I talk about "bad" and "good" days, I mean that from the common misconception I held that certain feelings were either "good" or "bad." I've learned differently now. But I use that language because it's most familiar to us. Yet, it's often because of this binary that we feel constrained. We're either one or the other. And because of this, that voice in our head becomes a blare-horn instead of a cheerleader, especially if we don't measure up to the preconceived notion of what we "should" be.

When my children were toddlers and getting to the age we felt they could watch a little television, we first turned to the classics, *Sesame Street* and *Mr. Roger's Neighborhood.* While the impact on my children is still to be determined, it is with certainty and clarity that those shows reignited my love of childhood. I was filled with the sense of community and kindness the characters on Sesame Street portrayed. I saw the calm, quiet way Mr. Rogers spoke to the camera, knowing he knew he was really speaking to the children *and* adults watching, and I felt like a child again. But even more than that, it transformed how I parented and taught.

I thought back to some of my tough days in the classroom. The days that needs were high and attitudes higher. I recalled words I said to children that weren't always positive. I thought about how I was hurting then, too. While it's not an excuse, it is a reality. Rewatching those episodes of *Mr. Roger's* gave me a new perspective. While not religious enough to ask "W.W.J.D," I did feel compelled to ask "W.W.M.R.D?" *What would Mister Rogers do?*

What would he do in those pressure cooker situations?

How would he handle parent conflict?

How would *he* speak to children?

Suddenly, I felt less shame for my bad days and rejuvenation for the ones ahead of me. I was going to change. I was going to change *me*.

When I felt stuck, angry, and wanted to scream at a six-year-old, I took a breath and asked myself, *What Would Mister Rogers Do?* An ease washed over me. A presence refocused me. It didn't solve the situation, but it bought me room. It allowed me space between the incident, the trigger, and how I wanted to respond. It gave me the gift of conscious decision.

When situations became more challenging, I felt out of control. Although I didn't want to ask "W.W.M.R.D," I did it anyway. It reminded me of the power I had at that moment. I could decide what was next, and moreover, I remembered my *why*.

We need that support—that safety harness—to know that when we're stuck in the mud and are having one of "those" days, we needn't worry that all our hard work will unravel. The good days don't pass because we've suddenly become incompetent or never had it from the start; they pass because it's in the nature of life: *Impermanence*. But there are things we can do to stay focused. And it comes back to your Why. *Why* are you doing this? *How* are you doing this? *What* will you do when it gets hard?

It's OK if you don't have those answers worked out just yet. I suspect by the end of this book, you will.

Because when it gets hard, and we all know it will get hard, we have to have a foundation to fall back on. In many ways, Mr. Rogers became mine. Like that strap on a treadmill that provides a layer of safety, remembering his philosophy held me when I would lose my footing. (Ironically, I don't use that treadmill strap when I exercise because I assume I won't slip.) But in life, in this work, I need that safety clip just as much as I need the buckles and the harnesses on a rollercoaster. I wouldn't dare dream of going on that ride without those supports! And yet, when we enter a classroom with only pedagogical knowledge, it's like trying to hop on a speeding treadmill and stay upright in a handstand. Perhaps that way of teaching used to work, but it doesn't anymore. Because the world has changed. We have changed. We have evolved. It's absolutely essential to be in touch with our feelings and vulnerabilities. To carry on as teachers, we need to know that we can have good and bad days.

And so it is that you have the power to have your *Beyoncé* days and eat your cake, too. Though, if you're starting to feel like this is all too much, breathe. I didn't get there in one day. I didn't get there in one year either. It's been a cumulation of trial and error. And boy, have I made some errors. More importantly, though, I've learned that even if you break down, you can build yourself back up.

Consider This:
- What "and" statements reflect your teaching experiences?
- How might you integrate the two paths into your days starting this week?

2

You've Been Up Against A Lot

We are all people with fears.

I hope you've spent some time reflecting on your Beyoncé days. Those days don't make us avoid the hard days but allow us to rejoice when the good is here. To feel the joy we so deserve. Still, for as great as those days are, we know we can't have them all the time. We will certainly still have "bad" days, and I will help you navigate through them, but bad *all the time* isn't healthy. It's unbalanced. I don't want us to keep pretending that everything's OK when it's not.

Teacher, you've experienced an insurmountable amount of pressure during the past few years. If you are tired, it's because it's been tiring. If you're sad, it's because it has been sad. If you're mad, it's because it's been maddening. While these past few years have had significant consequences, you and I both know we were already dealing with a lot before March 2020. Yes, it's been hard lately, but it's *always* been hard.

I was recently at a therapy appointment when the counselor referenced the "name it to tame it" work by Daniel J. Siegel and Tina Payne Bryson, co-authors of *The Whole Brain Child*.[4] That is precisely what we are doing here. We are naming what's been in front of us to better identify what is and what isn't ours to carry; this helps us notice our inner critic when it tells us we're not doing a good enough job. It's a way for us to say, "Wait a second. That's not true! Look here! I *am* doing a lot!"

When we're clued into what we've been holding, it makes space for us to grow grace and self-compassion in the areas we feel we've failed. It allows us to see it's impossible to do this work perfectly. In fact, you'll see perfect doesn't exist. When you shift your perspective to focus on what's caused your perceived failure (i.e., the too many bags you've been holding) versus the failure itself (i.e., the drop), you gain the emotional resilience to do the work that matters to you.

But how do we do it? How do we go from our fantastic, amazing Beyoncé days to breakdowns? Much like a pot of water on a stove doesn't go from cool to boiling instantly, neither do we. It's often an accumulation of hard days.

So, what do they look like? What do our hard days look like? What are we really facing on a day-to-day basis?

Let me know if it's something like this:

You wake up after five snoozes. You're not worried about getting to work late. You're concerned about what it will be like to go in feeling hollow.

Yesterday's afternoon is still replaying in your head:

You tried everything to get their attention: lights on, lights off, quiet voice, loud voice.

"Sit in your chair."

"No, stand up."

"No, you may not go to the office right now."

"Because."

"Remember, our whiteboards stay on the table. Eyes up here."

Your angst and irritation grow. You remind yourself to breathe, but all you can think about is how disorganized everything feels right now.

You threaten a loss of privilege to your classroom.

You see the looks on the faces of the kids who were listening and know that even as you mention this consequence, they're the ones who will miss out the most.

You do it anyway, against your better judgment, because what else is there to do right now?!

That helped for a little bit. But when it was time to transition to cleanup, your one friend didn't want to put away the pens. Frustrated by their partner's lack of help, the other kids in the group start putting the materials away themselves.

But that set off the storm.

Friend started grabbing for anything they could get their hands on. You rally the other kids to go to their spots, which they do, but it doesn't take long for them to get swirly and out of sorts while you're trying to help calm down this one.

You try to help *Friend*, but are only met with a barrage of "No." They run to the back corner.

You glance at the clock and see there are only 15 minutes until dismissal. That would be great if it weren't for the fact that no one's ready to go.

You call out a few directions and attempt to regain control.

At this point, *Friend* is now rolling on the floor along the back of the classroom. But they're not disturbing anyone else, so you take the moment to begin dismissal procedures.

Crap! You forgot to pass out snacks, AND it's Monday folder day.

Five minutes left.

You ask a dependable student to pass out the folders.

You look back at *Friend* because now they're squawking and pushing down chairs.

Two minutes until the bell rings.

Alright, everyone's almost all ready. *Wait, no, why did they stop? And why are those two getting out crayons?*

A lot can go wrong after this point; in my case, this is what followed in a setting in which dismissal procedures included families picking their children up directly from the classroom:

You hear the shuffling of feet in the hallway. Parents are beginning to line up at the door.

One minute.

Someone cries out because *Friend* just pinched them.

"ENOUGH!" you yell. And immediately sink down, knowing that it was loud enough for the parents to hear.

One pokes their head through the door.

"Hi, we'll be right out!," you say coolly.

"Jeeze, can't they just give me a minute?!" you think. *"It's only two minutes past dismissal."*

You scramble to get the kids and their belongings in enough order to release them.

Five minutes past the hour.

The parent pokes their head in again. The line has grown, and you now see the disappointment on *their* faces. Like parent, like child.

You want to call for help for *Friend*, but you know in doing so it will eat even more time up. Screw it, you're just going to start dismissing.

You try to regain composure when you open the door, but the disappointment lingering in the hallway hits you in the face.

Flushed and with concealed frustration, you say aloud, "Thank you for your patience." The first two parents try to ask about their kid's day, but you've left your body. The disassociation builds, and all you can muster is a "Yep."

Finally, all the students have been dismissed, even those going to after-care, but *Friend* is still in the room. They haven't cleaned up their stuff yet, and now they're just playing. While not as mad, you just don't have the emotional bandwidth to deal with this any longer. You want to ask for help, but you're already so embarrassed that you couldn't manage your class properly.

You are, however, tired and annoyed. You were planning to make all those copies after school. Instead, you're dealing with this during your prep time.

Eventually, you go across the hall to hail the help of your colleague.

Your coworker enters the room, and *Friend* listens the first time to everything they say.

Sigh. You die a thousand deaths while staring blankly at the wall ahead.

Was every day like this? No. But there were definitely enough that I've lost count.

It's worth noting that what was described above wasn't even a full day. The above scenario was 30 minutes. Yet, the weight could carry well into the next day.

Unfortunately, the reality is that situations like the one above weren't just happening once a day. Some days might have seen that on replay two- three- times per day, per week. Given that we are bombarded with scenarios like the one above for 6 hours—the length of the school day—it is no surprise that a classroom can become a boiler room.

How might this differ for you if you're a 5th-grade teacher? High school? How have your "bad" days changed as you became more experienced? If you've moved schools or districts, did you get more support in some buildings than others? What about it felt hard for you? What do you wish you could go back and tell yourself on those days?

Here is a note I wrote to myself the evening after one of my worst days.

I need nonjudgement.
I need acceptance that my classroom is a mess and that it's ok.
I need to know it will be ok.
I need a handle on my expectations.
I need acceptance of the present moment.
I need to let go of what I can't change.
I need to see joy in situations.
I need to use my voice to help others.
I need to know my limits and say what I need.
I need time and space to reflect.
I need time to have a balance to focus on me.

This was March 2018, four months after returning from maternity leave. I couldn't shoulder the pressure any longer. That night, I never wanted to see the inside of my classroom again.

Have you ever had that feeling? Maybe you're feeling it now. Maybe you've been asking yourself the same question I did: "Should I stay or go?"

I have been listening to you. I know you're tired.

The ongoing Pandemic, the heated political landscape, the consequences on curriculum, and the rise of acts of violence against Black people, Asians, and the Queer community—starting in 2020 alone—have undoubtedly created a cataclysmic avalanche of overwhelm and trauma.

I wasn't actively teaching during the Pandemic, nor did I experience the shift to virtual teaching, but I was swept away by dashed dreams, uncertainty about safety, and the insanity of having my life turned upside down. In Fall 2019, my husband and our two-year-old twin daughters moved from Oakland, California, to Vancouver, British Columbia. I was isolated in a new country, still trying to survive parenting twin two-year-olds. My isolation involved questioning my relationship with education, leading me to suddenly lose the identity I'd held on to for the previous eleven years.

Four months after our move to Canada, when things finally started to settle down from our transition, and I was *just* about to reenter the outside-of-home working world, everything shut down. I became more lost than I knew was possible. The light in me went off for a very long time, too.

You may not have had the privilege of entering into an existential crisis because people—other children and families—were counting on you. You didn't have the time to consider how to react. You went home on a Friday in March and were expected to completely change your approach by Monday. Rightfully, you probably *were* thinking about the children. And I'm sorry you weren't given time to think about you.

But you have been on my heart all along.

I couldn't have predicted how that note I scrawled to myself one late spring day several years ago would come back to serve as the basis for what I do now. How potent and true its words would still be today. Then, nestled in my blankets and pajamas, I had the emotional safety and clarity to write down what I really wanted. What I really needed. With distance from the incident that preceded it, I gave myself permission to speak the truth. Looking back, I can see how the me of 2020 and the one writing today needed to hear that same message. I believe you do, too.

I may not have been in the classroom, or the virtual classroom, during the Pandemic, but I hear you. I know what you've been up against.

You have been on a treadmill, going backward, carrying a jug atop your head while a screaming baby is strapped to you, a toddler clings to your leg, and a teenager sneaks out to see their friends. Your one hand that managed to be free is now having to decide between answering the call from the doctor or steadying yourself on the rail so you don't slip. Nope, it went to voicemail. Time to play phone tag and cue the hold music. Forget about lunch.

All the while, 30 faces stare back at you, wondering when you'll let them out to recess. Did I forget to mention you're also teaching a complex lesson with dodgy wifi? Inevitably, one person has to use the bathroom, two need to visit the nurse, and three think it's time to go home. And, wait a second, *where did Johnny go*? Of course, this is all metaphorical, but is it?

How often are we met with a dizzying amount of need?

And is there anything we can do about it?

Fortunately, I will help you. I hope to give you the care, compassion, and nurturing you need to let go of the weight you've been carrying and, in turn, help you replace your inner critic with a voice of courage, confidence, and kindness.

Unfortunately, working conditions have become so complicated in education that many cannot take the demands any longer. You may have seen this in your very own school. According to a Gallup poll conducted in 2022, K-12 teachers are the "most burnt-out profession in the United States."[5] Additional numbers from the Bureau of Labor Statistics showed that around "300,000 public school teachers and other related staff left the education field from February 2020-May 2022."[6]

Teaching has always been difficult, but it's become unsustainable. We have a right to be angry that this work we love so much and want to do cannot be done without consequences to our mental or physical health.

Hardworking professionals and experts are leaving the field of education because the game isn't fair.

Some say there isn't a teacher shortage but a shortage of *teacher care*—of caring enough about teachers to provide proper compensation, autonomy, and safety. Who wouldn't be upset about that?

Is this really how heroes are treated?

We receive gracious cards, mugs, flowers, and coffees from well-meaning parents and endearing children, notepads, and tote bags from people who want to show their thanks. Every election season, we hear platitudes about "bettering education for all" from policymakers. But are these gifts and gestures enough? Unfortunately not.

While true appreciation from a supportive parent or administrator has the potential to make our day go from bad to good or good to great, unfortunately, this is all we often get. Our cries of crisis are going unheard. The public *understands* that teachers "have a hard job that [they] could never do," but nothing is being done to actually change the policies that keep us struggling. The system keeps on ticking, and we're heroes because of it.

But maybe we don't want to be brave.

At the beginning of the Pandemic, the vocal appreciation for teachers and healthcare workers was the pot that could be heard worldwide. We were revered. Suddenly, every household understood what it was like to have to do it all.

March of 2020 was the first time the outside world faced the enormity of a teacher's task load. Suddenly, caregivers were more responsible for ensuring their child was reaching academic success.

It became very clear, very quickly, just how many obstacles teachers have been up against—how many balls we've been juggling. These include, but are not limited to, lack of space, materials, and preparation.

Over time, as virtual teaching became a staying reality, parents' and caregivers' decreasing bandwidth, busy schedules, and trying to hold the weight of surviving a pandemic clashed against the constant battle of also trying to teach human beings. Everyone was at their brink. And when it felt like it couldn't rain any harder, down poured the endless distractions, illnesses, and run-of-the-mill, albeit excited, developmental behaviors. These are all things that teachers contend with daily.

We stayed heroes long enough for everyone to forget why they called us that in the first place. In 2024, with kids back to pre-pandemic school models, it seems the public's gone quiet once again.

Hero, no more.

And the load hasn't become any lighter.

The *National Education Association* (NEA) defines teacher burnout "is a state of emotional, physical, and mental exhaustion caused by excessive and prolonged stress. In the context of education, it occurs when the demands of teaching exceed the resources available to cope with those demands."[7] In Chapter 7, we will examine this ever-present reality, including my own experiences of it within and outside the classroom.

Burnout is causing good teachers to leave the profession, yet those who stay also feel the heat. Up to 80% of teachers say that they've had to pick up duties and responsibilities to cover for staff shortages.[8] The problems are not getting smaller. They're only becoming bigger.

When we do not value teachers and provide them with liveable, sustainable compensation and working conditions, the beast begins to lose its buttons. And that's precisely what happened to me in March 2018, hours before I wrote the note at the beginning of this chapter.

With two hours left before dismissal, I struggled to make eye contact. I could barely look at my own reflection. My face was swollen and red. I couldn't see past my nose. The events of that afternoon churned in my head:

"Am I allowed to say that? Am I allowed to cry right now?" I thought to myself. The lights were dimmed; it was late afternoon. The kids had just returned from Music class. I was gearing up to teach a Culture Lesson. Only nothing was happening because no one was listening. My head spun at frantic speed. I could see the 29 kindergarten students sitting on the rug, but a two-way mirror suddenly appeared before me. I was in the room but out of body. I was at the head of my class, but I felt miles away from being their leader. To my left, five-year-

olds were flinging themselves on the floor; to my right, friends were poking their peers. I gave redirection after redirection, but nothing worked.

At first, I felt the anger. It started in the pit of my stomach and quickly shot to my hands, now balled, my fingernails pressed into my palms. Classroom management strategies were weaving through my head, and I was trying desperately to cling to one, the way people in those money machines make mad grabs for cash. It all felt like it was slipping away.

I wasn't in control.

Panic, worry, and tension grew and grew. Thoughts darted through my mind: *Do I yell? Do I wait? Do I stay silent? Do I get up and do something else? Can I quit right now?!*

"I can't do this, I can't do this, I can't do this," played on repeat. I thought those words were contained in my head, and then I realized I was actually saying them aloud, my body rocking back and forth. I knew it was now or never. Either I suck it all back in, or I just let it out. *"Can I let it out?"* I wondered. At this point, I couldn't stop the tears if I tried.

My co-teacher wasn't in the room then, but thankfully, another colleague came in and saw me at that exact moment. I looked at her with both relief and embarrassment. "I'm sorry, I can't do this," I managed to tell her. Without hesitation, she said, "It's ok, just go. I got this."

Walking down the hallway, I realized I didn't even know where I was walking to. All I knew was I had to get out of the classroom, and get out fast.

For the rest of that day, in March 2018, I stayed in my boss' office, afraid to return to my classroom. I was scared to see the children and more terrified to see any adults who may have seen me cry. I worried that my mistakes would get me in trouble. *How could I be so unprofessional?* I thought. *I can't believe this is my life right now. How did I let it get so bad?* Images of successful, talented teacher Christina flooded my brain, followed by the scenes of what just happened. The whiplash and disconnect between the reality of where I was and the expectation of where I thought I should be swallowed me whole.

Sitting in the poorly decorated office that looked as abandoned as I felt, I kept thinking about tomorrow. *What was I going to do tomorrow? I can't quit, right? That's crazy. But I can't take this either.* When my boss asked me what I needed, I was too afraid to say how I really felt: I didn't want to be there anymore. It had been the worst year ever.

I thought I had had it bad in 2014, but this was worse—this was hell's bigger, badder cousin called "postpartum." Also called "trying to return to work full-time with four-month-old twins at home." Also called, "and hating every moment you're away." I was trying to be both a good, brand-new mother and a good, old teacher. Called, "Christina loses her shit again."

This wasn't even my first year teaching or my fifth; it was my tenth. And it wasn't even the first time I called it "the worst year ever." The school year before my husband and I moved from Pennsylvania to California, I thought that *that* was my worst teaching year. And here I was, at the very school that had become a beacon after my last breakdown, now breaking down again.

What is wrong with me?

I was in a different state, teaching a different class, but I had the same agonizing feeling of wanting to be anywhere other than where I was at that moment. I wanted to be so far away from these troubles that they would have to send a search party to find me. Sadly, part of me desperately wanted to be found. I wasn't sure where the real me went. *Why did this have to happen again? I thought I was supposed to be getting better.*

That moment in the classroom was days and weeks of crushing defeat, resentment, and grief. However, I couldn't truly process any of it because I had so much on my plate. And it's only now, after time and therapy, that I have the words to articulate those experiences.

Interestingly, the more I learn about the children around me, including my own, the more I pick up information that I can apply to myself, things that were never taught at home or school. This is one way I reparent myself. When I transform myself, I can transform my teaching.

And learning about the nervous system from my child's therapist provided me with a shift I needed.

Like the children, youth, and adults around you, your internal processing center determines if you are safe all day long. When it detects a situation as unsafe, threatening, or challenging, you may *"fight, flee, or flop."*[9]

But sometimes, the pressure is so gradual we don't even realize it's intensifying. Before we know it, we're in boiling water.

I experienced this figuratively and literally.

One night, as I hovered over the stove to make mac n cheese, I watched the pot of water start out cool and calm. Of course, old wives tell us never to keep our eyes on a pot. And while it's true I was growing impatient, my fascination with what was happening grew faster. For the ten minutes it took for the water to go from cold to hot, hot to boiling, I remarked to myself that *this was a process.* Something made it this way. And, even when the heat was applied, it didn't go from zero to boiling in 60 seconds. It took continuous pressure. The longer the fire was applied, the more it heated up. Eventually, unable to contain itself, it swirled and popped with explosive force. The only thing that made it stop was a release of pressure—a decrease of heat.

Calm and then chaos.

So, why are we sending teachers back into the classroom and expecting them not to boil over? We haven't taken them off the stove. We haven't removed anything from their hot plates. Everything's still burning.

While I can't get rid of the fire, I can help you better handle the heat. In some places, maybe we can even turn it down.

This is also why the work of trauma researchers and therapists, like Lisa Dion of the Synergetic Play Therapy Institute, plays a crucial role in helping us support the children in our classroom and our own biological needs as well.

Like the children in our room, our adult bodies also respond to situations based on our perception of them. It does not matter if it's an actual physical attack on the body; what's important in nervous system regulation is how a situation or challenge is perceived.[10]

For students and staff who've experienced trauma, both big T and little t, being in the classroom all day can be like hovering in Hell, stuck in a pot of scorching liquid. Eventually, without the proper support, someone will erupt, which we often see in classrooms today. Arguably, it's what we've always seen, but now we have more widely accessible research and language to support it.

For teachers, and for teachers who are also parents, your nervous system is a circuit board on Speed. All day long, for six hours at school, and when you come home, your body assesses the stimuli around you. Depending on what you're up against, you can become activated. Your body may need more input. You notice you may need to twist or talk or sing or chew. You may become easily overwhelmed or more aggressive and short-fused. You'll want to argue or move things around.

Conversely, your dysregulation might warrant a binge session on the couch. (Hot Cheetos and Pepsi for me, please.) You might feel like a brick or excessively tired. You'll be drawn to cloak your body in comfort. Think hoodies, weighted blankets, et al. Or, in the case of flee, or "flight" as it's often referenced, you'll want to run. To get out of there fast. Perhaps the fantasy of boarding a plane and never looking back comes to mind.

The conflict is too much. The tension is too high. And there's not enough help.

These levels, or symptoms, of activation, are also what the children in our class come in contact with each day. For children who are more prone to anxiety, hypersensitivities, and/or live(d) with *Adverse Childhood Experiences*, their arousal state may be more rapidly and frequently "on edge."[11] *Happy wife, happy life?* More like, "on edge student, on edge adult."

How many on-edge kids does it take to get to the center of a teacher?

While there were days and years when I felt the heat more than others, most of my time in the classroom was relatively stable. I wasn't breaking down every day. In actuality, the everyday minutia and impossible grind led to my eventual eruption, not the eruption itself. I was the proverbial pot on the stove, still and then sudden.

The goal of noticing your nervous system symptoms is that you can more easily regulate yourself. I've had many years where this was not a problem for me. But, when the needs around me became higher than I could manage—when the pot got too hot—my system came under attack. And I wasn't even aware I was in survival mode.

Now I can see that being unable to communicate clearly, maintain eye contact, or feel grounded enough to make conscious choices—all hallmarks of a regulated system—didn't make me a bad teacher. It was my body's way of protecting me. It was trying to communicate in a language I couldn't understand, and I didn't have the tools to fend for myself.*12

So, why is learning about the nervous system crucial?

When we prepare teachers for the emotional velocity that awaits while charging them with the awareness of the present moment, we can help them see they work hard every day, and some days, it still doesn't feel like enough. We can validate this experience for others and validate it for ourselves because this is human nature.

We can better hold the good and the bad. We can interrogate a thought that tells us we're not enough and replace it with a more helpful one: *It may not feel like enough, but it will still be enough. We are still enough.* Then, we can guide them and ourselves to the next moment. Or as longtime writer and author Emily P. Freeman shepherds, to just *the next right thing.*13

On those hard days, we can begin to see this does not make us a failure, nor does it mean we care about the children any less. In fact, some may argue being able to hold these boundaries and realistic expectations shows how much we *do* care.

It also allows us to live in *The Land of And.*

We can love what we do and hate other parts of it. You can like being a teacher and only sometimes like what you teach. You can enjoy your students and still be displeased with certain behaviors and personalities—even the ones out of their control. This is normal. You, too, are a human being.

This isn't a book about how to teach better. It's a book about how to live better. It's a book about how to live better when teaching is your life. How you can be kinder, gentler, and more forgiving of yourself and your process so you can show up as your whole human self in the classroom. By doing so, you also give permission to others around you to do the same. You are also more accepting when you see staff and students in distress. By recognizing your own inherent worth and humanity, you can see that vulnerability does have a place in the classroom. It should have a seat at the table. When you can find more ways to express your feelings—mindfully and authentically—you give yourself grace for when you miss the mark. You recognize that missing the mark may be a mistake, but it's not a failure. You see that what you put in still has rewards. You are the reward. You are the prize you've been waiting for.

There is so much that you've been up against, teacher. This work aims to identify the internal and external pressures facing you and your colleagues. What's shared here won't necessarily make them go away, but the goal is for you to see that you do not need to carry the weight of the world on your back. Though I know that you have. I have, too.

Parent or not, you've been shouldering more than you should. These past few years have cracked an already fragile foundation. Furthermore, they've put a spotlight on the systems that do not serve us.

I come to you at the intersection of knowing what it's like to be inside the classroom and what it's like to be out. My feelings of overwhelm, inadequacy, and constant belief that I should "do better because I know better" serve as the basis of this book. I want us to dive into the external factors that have been playing against us and our colleagues. As someone who values professional development and continuing education, I'd be remiss if I didn't also acknowledge the areas I've gotten it wrong. Naming those uncomfortable feelings of shame helps us move forward. It's how we pick up Grace.

Teachers have endured so much in the past few years, and for many, their entire careers, so I knew that I needed to speak to what causes us to lose heart in this profession. It often takes more than it gives, and I want to change that.

Teacherhood is a word I've been using to define what it means to be a teacher. It encapsulates the identity one claims while teaching and honors and examines the experiences one has because of it. It is akin to states and associations such as motherhood, parenthood, womanhood, and sisterhood. Teacherhood includes both internal and external factors and can vary from person to person. There are both positives and negatives to teacherhood. One can like being a teacher without liking all the parts of it.

Every school I worked at was beautiful, and every school had problems. While certain situations made me want to pursue work elsewhere, my struggles at each one fell into two categories: internal and external.

And, teacher, there were some things we were never meant to take on. Throughout these pages, let's name those barriers. We have to know what we're up against before we can do something about it. Naming what's hard might make us feel overwhelmed at first, but it also sets us free. We can breathe through the tension. That's why I'm walking with you as you discover more about our profession and your place in it.

Check in with yourself. How are you doing? Do you need to get up? Stretch? Grab some tea? Hot Cheetos?

Next, we'll look at how our life transitions have changed us over the years, including how our role as educators has shaped our identity. We'll also see what can happen when our roles and identities shift. How do *you* navigate these changes? Do some come to mind right now? Let's go there.

> **Consider This:**
> * What goes through your mind on your bad days?
> * How would you define your Teacherhood experience? What is true for you?

3

It's Hard Because It's Hard

Anytime I've judged another's situation, it's come back tenfold in my own life.

Changing schools and changing placements are some of the most prominent shifts teachers experience, but they're not the only ones that affect us. Within those macro-changes, micro-ones occur, too. Depending on the switch—for example, if you go from Grade 5 to Kindergarten—you may need to learn an entirely new curriculum. Perhaps even a new way of relating to children. Not to mention getting acquainted with a new set of grade-level colleagues! As a result of these changes, you may have more questions than answers as you look at what's in front of you.

It's my goal to share what makes transitions in education so tricky and provide an alternative way of thinking about our challenges when we're in them. Moreover, I wish to acknowledge the effects of more significant life transitions—such as moving states, changing your relationship status, entering parenthood, questioning your identity, and, as we all saw, world pandemics—can have on us.

What's inside comes out, and what's outside comes in. As we learned from the last chapter, we have to name what's been in front of us.

I write as a mother and educator who's been in private, public, and charter school classrooms from Pennsylvania to California. I've worked in traditional settings and Montessori. I was also granted a bird's eye view of early childhood operations when I sat as an Executive Board President of a Preschool. The trajectory of my educational path, let alone my mothering one, has profoundly changed me. It's led to some of my greatest joys and my deepest hurts.

You don't need to be a mother or a parent (or female) to understand what many teachers are up against, but may these stories and snippets from my life offer you the compassion and empathy you need to move forward. May it tune you into the path others walk and grant us all a little more humanity along the way. May you learn the grace and self-compassion you need when transitioning.

So, take a moment now and think about some of the transitions that come to mind. What have you traversed thus far? Can you categorize them into "school-related" and "home-related?" How have they intersected?

Who are you right now because of those transitions? What makes up your identity?

Knowing this will help you see the impact of your career and life changes on you. And if you're anything like me and *know* whenever you're "in transition," but don't let yourself *feel* the transition, this is the chapter for you.

Sometimes, I'm still quite shocked at the number of big transitions I've made, considering I eat a sandwich and yogurt every day for school lunch. There's safety and predictability in knowing what to expect. Unfortunately, when it came to three of my most notable transitions, my high expectations and need for routine didn't leave any room for the contents to shift.

My first notable transition was in 2013 when I returned to teach in a traditional setting after a Montessori one. The second was in 2017 when I first had to make space for teacher-me and parent-me. And the most challenging was in 2019, when our family moved to Canada four months before the COVID-19 pandemic, and I went from teacher to stay-at-home-*what am I doing with my life*? What made all of those transitions so difficult was the belief they were going to be perfect. Ignoring the complexities of life, I believed my transitions would be smooth. When they got bumpy, hit roadblocks, and completely crashed on the side of the road, I didn't know what to do with myself.

Before them, I could have *told* you they'd be challenging, but somewhere, I kept the naive thought that somehow I'd be immune. Maybe *you* could experience hardship, but I wouldn't.

The high expectations I set for myself didn't leave any room for detours or destruction.

So when they came, I didn't look at my situation for the difficulty it was. I blamed myself.

And why shouldn't I? I trained for this!

As a student, I was always near the top of my class. School and all that came with it was easy for me. I understood what was expected, and I followed suit. I liked to do well. However, when I got to high school and was surrounded by AP classes and students who received perfect SAT scores, I stopped feeling as bright as my parents and grandparents always said I was. I graduated with honors and was proud of my work ethic, but

I felt mediocre. Knowing there were people better than me out there made me feel small and wilted compared to them.

But things changed when I started college. Perhaps it was due to that collegiate preparatory school I attended, but suddenly, I felt back in my domain. School and I were best buds again.

When I finally began my education courses at Edinboro University of Pennsylvania, now called PennWest Edinboro, I felt on top of the world. Despite the mediocrity I felt up to this point, this new thing—teaching—felt right. I *got* the material. During my second year, one of the first courses I took was "Teaching Children's Literature." I loved every moment of it. I recall sitting in my grandparents' old living room, where my father lived at the time, and delighting in crafting a file folder game based on *The Polar Express* by Chris Van Allsburg. The movie version, featuring Tom Hanks, had just been released in theaters, which threw excitement in the air. I sat on the blue carpet, coloring in the silver bell and writing down follow-up questions to the text. I looked up at my Uncle's shiny, black piano—a staple of my grandparent's house—and saw my joy beaming back at me. I felt so proud. I couldn't believe I was actually doing teacher work and that it could be this fun and intuitive!

And I wasn't there to mess around like some of the other students. This work was pressing and important to me from the start. It gave me a new way to see myself. I knew I would give it my all, and I did. In 2008, I graduated Summa Cum Laude and was awarded the Elementary Education Award.

I might not have felt good at a lot of things, but I knew I was good at teaching.

However, as great as my schooling was, I learned a harmful binary: there's a right way to be a teacher and a wrong way.

And I desperately wanted to be on the side of right. Good teaching, bad teaching. Right teaching, wrong teaching. For the kids or the teacher. It was easy to see what my professors expected of us: demonstrate the knowledge, skills, and disposition of a good teacher.

For me, a good teacher understood how to manage her class. She didn't use basal readers but explored literacy through authentic children's literature. She went straight to the source of the material to glean lesson elements. She rarely used worksheets, and if she did, they were ones she created. Manipulatives were a must. She also knew that Lesson Planning, Curriculum Mapping, and Alignment were vital. A good teacher also demonstrated care and compassion for her students: she didn't yell, she didn't embarrass kids, and she most definitely kept her cool even if her room was on fire. Everything was for the children and for the school.

Furthermore, a good teacher modeled, scaffolded, and modeled some more. She held high expectations of her students and made the processes clear for the learners to learn.

For me, the pinnacle of great teaching was successfully implementing guided reading groups and strong, smooth Reading and Writing Workshops, where you were aware of each child's level and needs. It was important for me to be the best.

While I did not always produce on this end, I also knew it was important to be able to control your class and patiently and expertly manage their emotional outbursts. As a teacher, you were expected to do all of this and to do all of it well.

Those were not the exact lessons my professors taught. Still, I deduced such messages through my coursework, observations, and what I would later know as my internal dialogue and perfectionism. And when I couldn't do it well, I didn't know what to do.

One night, while student-teaching in late Autumn of 2007, I stayed up for hours past my usual bedtime to curate the perfect lesson. I was being observed the following morning by my esteemed advisor, the late Dr. Virginia McGinnis, and I wanted everything to be excellent. I couldn't leave room for error. My office floor was barely visible—papers, markers, tape, and reference texts were scattered about as I prepared lesson materials for the next day. You couldn't take a step without risk of tripping. When I finally finished and felt satisfied with the work, I had no energy to clean it up. I left a sign on the door for my roommates that read: "Disaster Area. Will Clean Later!" I sunk into bed at 2 a.m., exhausted but with a mind still racing over details.

Teaching became my new identity. I loved the organization and professionalism of it all. My deep love of play and admiration of children often made teaching feel effortless. Even when uncertain about what to do, I felt driven to find a solution. I was determined to keep trying. I was committed to this work. I carried the pride of my undergraduate degree and University training into student teaching and beyond. I knew I had prepared well. And I was ready to prove it. I wanted to give kids the education they deserved.

However, for much of my life and career, I believed it was imperative to like all my students and that all of them should like me. This belief—that I only unlearned through therapy and the gracious sharings of teachers, visionaries, and psychologists on the internet—made me feel responsible for how others felt. Therefore, it only made sense to me to feel like I was also responsible for teaching them everything. I had to be everything to them. My portfolio cover read, "Committed to Success." I believed that.

It didn't matter that some needs might have been out of my scope and experience. Because they were mentioned in my undergraduate and graduate courses, I assumed that I had to meet them 100% of the time. This was my training, after all. Anything less was unacceptable.

Yet, the reality was I couldn't. I didn't. It was impossible for me to do that. This cross between the external pressures of what others expected of me and the internal pressures of what I expected of myself was indecipherable. To me, I just called it *responsibility*. These were my *responsibilities*: to address each student's needs, no matter what. The logical knowledge of my skill set bumped up against the emotional one of believing that I had to achieve perfection, which left me in a constant tug-of-war with myself. I didn't want to fail anyone, no less myself.

What have you carried with you from your teacher training? What would you change knowing what you do now? Perhaps you can start by reflecting on why you chose education in the first place and what beliefs and values you brought to the field.

In addition to my passion for working with youth, I chose education as my career path because it was straightforward. With a teaching degree, I knew what to do: get a teaching job. There was little room for variation in the best way possible. I didn't have to think about what kind of job I'd do had I chosen a Biology degree. Teaching would provide long-term stability because the job's parameters were outlined and completed within specific months. It didn't seem like education jobs were going anywhere.

Wrong. I tasted my first major transition during my third year of teaching. The district I worked for announced a budget crisis. On top of building restructures and new classroom configurations because of the cutbacks, all teachers with three years or less would be furloughed.

This was 2011, a few months after I began work towards my Master's degree and four months before I found myself in an entirely new educational model because of this transition.

While I do believe a career in education can provide structure and stability, we would be remiss to ignore the changes that happen within us and around us and the effect it has on our classroom experiences. Not to mention what happens when we fail in the roles we hold so dearly.

After the furlough news hit my district, I began applying to different schools and districts frantically, albeit confidently. Technically, my job in the Lake Erie School District was held, and I could be "called back" whenever their finances turned, but I didn't want to wait around and be unemployed.

I pressed on with my Master's program and began the interview process.

Ultimately, I got hired at Erie Montessori School, EMS, knowing very little about the Montessori curriculum. This was the first place that sent me in a new educational direction. Literally, too.

In the summer of 2011, I completed my seven-week summer training at the Center for Montessori Teacher Education in Queens, NY. Before I truly left, I was getting far away from Erie. I see now how I was untangling physically and emotionally from my 'home district' without really realizing it.

Entering the world of Montessori was eye-opening. The beauty and order of the lesson presentations touched me at a sensorial level, much like the curricular area of the same name. I was mesmerized by how simple and complex the philosophy and lessons were. I couldn't believe there were such lessons as handwashing and rug rolling, all things that lead to concepts of print. Still, to this day, the sound of water slowly trickling into a ceramic pitcher takes me back to that summer in Queens, where I completed my training. I was in awe.

And I was angry. As a well-educated and well-prepared educator, I couldn't believe that I didn't learn more from this teaching philosophy in college. Maria Montessori's alternative approaches, along with Waldorf and Reggio styles, usually only received a byline to the more respected teachings of Balanced Literacy, Classroom Management, and Differentiated Instruction. The former were often accompanied by a mere description of "child-centered approaches."

It's funny now writing these words. Had we examined these other styles of teaching, we would have been given another solution to meeting the needs of students. Yet they weren't even topics of conversation in my school of education. I was also angry to learn that Montessori, for the most part, is private. Montessori schools often come with a hefty price tag that rivals college tuition. I was angry that this amazing way of teaching was not accessible to the masses. I was thankful I'd be teaching at a public one.

Nonetheless, the academic scope and sequence of the Primary 3-6 program also went further than anything I had seen in the Kindergarten curriculum. Once I got over the shock that students aged three to six in the Primary program could learn high-level multiplication and division, I could also see that one part of the success of these programs was being able to work with children from the age of three, and in some cases, two and a half. In a typical Montessori setting, teachers work with children on a three-year cycle, guiding them and observing them as they reach various developmental stages, or as Montessori called them, sensitive periods.[14] The curriculum is spread out over three years, with one of the hallmarks of multi-age classrooms being that older and younger students learn from each other. Considering that most school teachers only have students for one academic year, it made sense that private Montessori models were successful: teachers got to work with students earlier and for more extended periods— something the traditional school system does not allow.

After I completed my training, I thought about how I would take a curriculum meant to be spread over three years and condense it into one tiny Kindergarten year. Many public, primary Montessori classrooms only enrolled kindergarten-age students due to licensing restrictions and preschool regulations.

On top of that, because my school was a public one, I would need to align the Montessori lessons with the state standards. But I felt up for the challenge. I was excited to take this newly learned information and implement it in my new classroom. At the same time, I started to imagine how great it would be to take these learnings back to the traditional school I came from.

And then that opportunity came.

Two years after working at Erie Montessori School, my former district called back the teachers who'd been furloughed, and I decided to return.

On paper, it seems like a straightforward decision, but weighing the pros and cons brought much turmoil. *Do I stay or do I go?* I found myself asking this question again almost ten years later. While I was discontent with my professional development at EMS, the two years there were the calmest of my career; returning to my first teaching school in the LESD after the furlough callbacks was complicated.

One of the main reasons I decided to return to my home district of LESD (besides a salary raise) was to see if I could make Montessori work in a traditional school. It was always on my mind since attending my summer training through CMTE in 2011. Having the opportunity to return to my first school placement, where I started my career, and to be able to bring new insights and ways of teaching with me pushed me to make that year successful. Because I decided to resign from EMS after the "callbacks," I put so much pressure on myself to have a positive year back at the district. And by Day 3, I regretted that decision.

Have you ever been there? Have you ever wished or hoped for something only to find out that the reality didn't meet your expectations? What about when that happens in the classroom?

One reason transitions can be so difficult is that I expect things to stay the same in my new setting. I expect everything that was will still be, just with this new thing tacked on. Because I looked forward to its arrival, I thought there was no way for me to fail. Especially because I chose it.

Yet, there I was, angry and defeated all of the time. I spent my evenings, weekends, and half-hour lunch breaks ruminating on all my decisions. When I had left the district, I had a reasonable class size of 20 students (would you believe that in my first year teaching kindergarten, I only had 15! I was too naive to appreciate it!), but when I returned to LESD, my class roster hovered around 28.

Additionally, for the previous two years, I had grown accustomed to working with a co-teacher or Teacher Assistant, as is common practice in Montessori classrooms. Back in the district, I returned to being the sole educator. With more responsibilities and fewer adults to spread out the work, burnout consumed me.[15]

Every day after school, I collapsed into a ball of sorrow and misery. My husband tried to be supportive as best he could, and he tried to remind me of how empowering it had been to stand up to my boss in salary negotiations, but all I could see now were the mistakes I had made.

I experienced whiplash like no other. Something that felt so right a few weeks prior, attempting to bring Montessori mainstream, felt wrong and misplaced and utterly overwhelming in this different setting. I often questioned if attempting to instill Montessori values, routines, and practices, such as children using materials on a "work rug" or having "choice within limits," would backfire. I worried that I'd be setting the students up for failure when they went off to Grade 1. "If I do this, but no one else is on board, then is this the right thing?" I often pondered. And then, with more doubt, "Why am I even doing this?" looped in my brain.

I was frustrated that I couldn't stick to one thing. I was frustrated the kids didn't seem to pick up on Montessori. The cloud of doubt hung over me as I weighed how to bridge two different educational philosophies.

Perhaps you find yourself here. Have you ever had an opportunity to combine your previous teaching experiences? If so, what went smoothly? What challenges presented themselves?

I used to wonder what teachers who'd been around a while thought about the "phonics wars" and whatever other topics became circular debates. I'd wonder what it felt like for them to see the car go around the block, perhaps twice or even thrice during their career. I wondered what they thought of the back and forth and where they stood. I feel like we're in that space again.

It is quite possible that, as a person living on this planet and in the sub-world of education, you will discover that the practices you have used will no longer be valid.

Of course, it's not fun to realize we've used instruction that no longer stands up or, worse, harms; however, if we are committed to seeking resources and ways of being that restore and work towards a better future for all, then that's the best we can ask for. Maybe that's all we're asking for.

I'm not saying this is always an easy pill to swallow. In fact, every time I've gone to write this section, my body has tensed up a bit.

But we can give ourselves grace. It's OK for you to change your mind about curriculum. It's OK to not know. Knowing who you are in this moment as an educator puts you on the path of moving forward.

It gives you an opportunity to assess your priorities.

It allows you to revisit your values.

And, if your life looks drastically different than it did a few years ago, you gain the ability to stitch together those seismic shifts.

We can ask ourselves, "How do I still honor what I know to be true and valid when I've evolved so much?" On the flip, "How might I return to my roots to find strength and identity?"

Whether questioning literacy instruction, dismantling systemic racism, or raising the next generation of learners, I'm confident we will continue fighting for what's best for children, backed by passion and science.

Rather than fill with dread over our shortcomings, may we find the peace offered to us in seeing ourselves anew, in believing in ourselves despite the unknown.

And I say that not because I want arrogance to remain in attendance but because I don't want shame settling in. We can't move through our learning process while we are stuck in shame.

Instead, we can allow the learning to change us.

But I didn't know that back in 2013. Instead, I pushed against what intuitively came to me. Beyond my doubt over my capabilities, being away from a traditional educational setting made me realize how overstimulating such a setting had become for me. In 8th grade, our class took a trip to the Rock & Roll Hall of Fame museum in Cleveland, Ohio. I recall one of my classmates proudly buying a shirt that read, "If it's too loud, you're too old." Right then, I declared myself old!

Fast forward a decade: *Oh,* the noise! The minimalist Montessori environment that I grew accustomed to, which is often what appeals to many parents when they consider enrollment, clashed with the sensory overload of the traditional room. Everything was so loud all of the time! From loud-speaker announcements to talking to others from across the room to the visual smorgasbord of posters, word walls, and anchor charts, it caught me off-guard. I wanted to rip everything off of the walls. And I did.

The shame I felt for my own behavior, including the disdain I felt for a place I used to call home, further alienated me.

Upon preparing this section, I realized I had a prior experience that articulated how heavily this transition weighed on me. Toward the end of my Master's in Reading program, I took a writing class. I wrote one paper about what it feels like when you can't go back home—when the home you grew up in is no longer there, figuratively and in some ways, literally.

I was 27 then and had been living on my own, out of my mom's house, for almost a decade. It was mid-October, a few months after my wedding, when I heard the news that the father of my childhood best friend passed away. I was still furloughed, working at EMS, and nestling into married life. I didn't visit my old neighborhood much, but I had no hesitation going to pay my respects.

On the afternoon of the funeral, all of my former neighbors were there, many of whom still lived on the street where I grew up, my brothers included. It was a mini-reunion. Being in that space with people I hadn't had much contact with, but all seemed so connected to each other, made it feel like an absolute time warp. Everything looked the same but felt different. I could see them, but it wasn't clear where I stood. I realized then, and after completing that essay, that home stopped feeling like home. I wasn't sure where my home was anymore.

That's what it felt like when I returned to the Lake Erie School District for the 2013-2014 school year after spending two years away at EMS. Truthfully, I wasn't sure what I would do if I ever got that callback. But when it came, I did what I felt best. I accepted my "old" position back and resigned from EMS.

But, as you saw, whatever eagerness I held quickly melted away on my first day back to LESD. It looked the same. It smelled the same. But it was not the same place I had left in 2011. And I realized I wasn't the same, either.

I wasn't sure who I was. Was I more Montessori? Was I more traditional? And who is "Mrs. Lindvay?" Last time I was at this school, I still had my maiden name, Ms. Coffey (and at EMS, I went by Miss Christina). Shame and doubt replaced my confidence as an educator.

I avoided eye contact with colleagues, teachers whom I called friends only years before. I was afraid they would see right through me. I was afraid and worried they *were seeing* right through me. They could see the *bad teacher* I told myself I was despite attempting to appear collected on the outside. The self-judgment piled up. I didn't like how I was acting towards kids. Kids who I wanted to help, but now only made me want to pull my hair out. I was beyond annoyed that the student behaviors were more than I could handle. I was embarrassed and hated going to work each day. This was not at all the teacher I trained to be. Cognitive dissonance swirled. Tension ate me for breakfast, lunch, and dinner.

All I could feel was pain and uncertainty in what I was doing. None of my plans were working. And, just as I would come to feel those years later in 2018, in California, several months postpartum, I felt even more shame and embarrassment when I thought about how the other adults in the school now saw me. I could barely look at myself during this time.

As a teacher, it felt like my greatest pride to be able to handle all that came my way. To fill all *who* came my way. In fact, there was not much I felt I couldn't handle.

That belief followed me into motherhood, too. When I learned I was expecting twins, I leaned on my training as a teacher to help me build structure. I held on to the belief I could juggle the needs of more than one kid *because I had done it before.* But I see now a lot of that was protection and ego. I couldn't admit to myself I couldn't do it all. Truthfully, it probably would have shattered my confidence. And I needed that to face what was in front of me.

And right now, teacher, I know there's so, so much in front of you.

When I decided to write this book, I had the teachers of 2020 on my mind. Overwhelmed was an understatement. When I thought about it more, I realized that for as hard as those Pandemic years were (and believe me, they were HARD), our feelings of inadequacy and shame were already woven throughout our profession. From changing placements to weighing different educational models, we've racked up enough stress to last a lifetime.

Thankfully, there are things I've learned since my most challenging years that are helping to clear the way. Things I've learned since stepping away from education have given me a path back to it. We're on that path right now, noticing our feelings and naming what's here.

With even greater distance from the day, I wrote that *Note to Self* in the last chapter. I've been able to see what made that season, and others like it, so strenuous.

I was in an identity and transitional limbo again. Trying to work full-time while my twin babies were at home with the nanny was not working out. It was so hard to care for other people's children when I was still learning how to care for my own. I had nothing left to give to my students, and when I arrived home, I felt like I was lacking there, too. My capacity was nowhere where it used to be. All I could see around me was lack and failure. I was on a postpartum survival schedule of sleep-feed-work-pump-feed repeat. On top of trying to find my old teacher self, I was looking for what it meant to be a new mother.

It is also important to state that I held this belief about my larger-than-life role in education long before I was a parent. My years of struggle also existed apart from my parenthood experiences. You don't need to be a parent to understand the ramifications of big life changes. Teachers of all genders, races, creeds, ages, and (non)parental statuses face similar challenges and experience changes such as moves, illness, or job loss.

Do any come to mind for you right now?

As much as we might not like to think about it, we are all impacted by systems that push against their people.

Unfortunately, when I was in the thick of it, when there were factors outside of my control—such as a teacher furlough or the timing of an offer—it was difficult for me to remain grounded. When my life circumstances changed—when I became a mother, when I moved—and the ground beneath me began to shake again, I didn't have the capacity or balance to create the classroom space I wished to see. The needs piled up, and I collapsed.

Writing these words here has helped me understand why those moments felt so painful. It's also helped me see what was happening under the radar.

Each time I left a school because of being overwhelmed, I had moments when I was angry at that particular location, but more specifically, I was angry at the system. I was angry with how unsupported we were regarding class size and the ability to serve all of our students' range of needs properly.

Grief came from not getting what I wanted and needed.

Part of the pain was that it wasn't always like this. At one point, my time in Pennsylvania with my first district felt like home. In all senses of the word, it was home. It was also where I attended K-12. It hurt a lot to lose that connection—first through furlough and then by choice. Then, in 2014, living in California, my tenure at Montessori School of Oakland, MSO, was like a springboard for my spirit to emerge. It felt like a beacon after my prior rough year. I found my footing and quickly folded into the staff. My time there, working with my friends, was a genuine soul expansion. It's what made it all the more difficult when I knew I had to leave after the postpartum breakdown in Spring 2018.

I changed once again.

And so did the system. Just not for the better.

It is never an easy decision to leave a school. There are colleagues you will miss, families you've grown connected to, and who wants to willingly pack up a lifetime of classroom materials?! But having the ability to experience different school settings in different states allowed me to see the struggles and strengths of each one. Beyond that, having space completely away from the classroom afforded me a privilege that I recognize many of you have not been able to take. It would be inaccurate of me to dismiss that privilege, *and* I realize it's also what's given me the perspective to be right here with you.

Today, I can see how my identities, while confusing at times, have also given me strength. Parenthood has humbled me in all of the ways teaching couldn't.

Each shift in my identity brings a new layer of perspective on the world, a new way to see my place in it, a new way to find ways to connect the loose threads, and a new way to place bows where they're needed.

Yes, it can create doubt for a period of time (impermanence), but I'm also learning to live in the waters that sway me, to trust they're taking me to the right shore, to understand that the current may take me far away, but I can return home—even if that takes some time.

How might, or how have, your identities and life transitions banded together to create the amazing human you are?

Where are you now? Are you in a position you love? Have you finally landed your dream job? Or are you in a period of waiting, in limbo, feeling like you're far from home? Are you on the brink of big change, or have you just settled into one?

I've experienced all of those states. Let me lead you to how we can ground ourselves when transitions and life throw us curveballs, when our expectations don't meet our reality. Even if we can't hold this for all our days, let me offer you a path forward. Let this carry you somewhere new.

Our identities will continue to change over time if we let them. This can be a good thing, too. If you'd asked me ten years ago if I'd be living a sober life now, I would have said, "No way!" Nor did I ever think I'd have twins! Or live in Canada! But here I am.

And there you are.

While all transitions cannot be avoided, we can at least offer ourselves grace when we're in them. We can be more realistic about our expectations for ourselves. We can reach out to others who may have walked a similar path. Simultaneously, we can find safety and assurance within ourselves. And we can be more willing to trust that even if we fall, we can get back up.

You may be surprised who you meet when you come back up for air.

In these years out of the classroom, freedom came for me. I started to see who I was besides being an educator. My image of what an educator could be shifted. It grew. It expanded. It started to make room for the person I am—the person I've always been.

Those of you who fight against yourself can understand the joy it is to finally come home, to be at peace, to love who you are inside and out, and to see *You*, to truly see and accept You.

It's taken me a while to get here. Admittedly, I'm still on my way. (I think we always will be). It's also something I have to actively choose. Self-compassion and grace don't come naturally to me. But I am choosing to believe that the more I seek them, the more I rely on the power of showing myself kindness and forgiveness, I will be restored. I can't go back to the other side.

And I know I'll have my hard days. We all will. I am not expecting this work to be perfect. I've learned that mistake the hard way. For so long, I tended to believe that just because I knew something—some really great, awesome, powerful truth—I'd be free to swim in its glory for the rest of my days. Wrong!

The knowledge is only good for as long as I practice it. Like the German language I learned in high school and college: if you don't use it, you'll lose it. We are human. As frustratingly beautiful as that is. Some of these tools will work for a time, and then you'll need new ones. I'm sure you're using some right now. Can you name them? In fact, share what works for you. We'll all be the wiser for it.

Allow learning to change us.

We can see ourselves in a new light. We can give ourselves time to heal, to grieve, to heal again. We can return to the path as often as needed, even if our knees are shaky and the waters below us murky. We can put two feet down and be present to where we are. That's courage on a small scale.

While I hope it helps you see how much power you have as a teacher, it's always been about you, the individual, first. It's about helping you see you are more capable than you give yourself credit for. It's about reminding you that life transitions are going to change you, but that doesn't mean you're out for the count. You may need a little more time.

And this can't happen overnight—it won't happen overnight. It will happen in small bits, taken lightly, and with patience. I know you are capable of it. If I can do it, so can you.

I was at the end of my rope, in despair, in fits and pits of rumination and regret, and today, I am here writing to you.

You will always be the one this work is for, whether you're in the classroom or not. Let's keep on.

> **Consider This:**
> - Which transitions of yours have been the most positive? Which have been the most challenging? How might the *Land of And* help you see where "both" exists?
> - What would you tell a teacher friend about to embark on one of those transitions?

4

You Don't Have to Do This Work Perfectly

I did the best I could with the information I had at the time.

A s outlined in the last chapter, I often dismissed the changes around me and believed I should carry on unscathed. Because I believed that I should be able to do it all, I didn't leave any room for when I couldn't.

The intensity of my high expectations peaked in 2020.

After moving to a new country, half-dealing with the news of my mom's recent cancer diagnosis, and having a rough go at transitioning to stay-at-home-parenting twins—atop a pandemic and civil rights upheaval—the volume of my inner critic turned to max. I wasn't sure where I stood anymore. At the end of the prior school year, I questioned my place in education. I wasn't sure how to turn my vision of transforming education into reality. Rather, I thought I was on my way, and then life hit hard. Thoughts of regret and refrains of "shoulda, coulda, wouldas" echoed in my ears.

When struggling with how to parent my children—where a few months prior I had no problem—I constantly thought,

"I should be able to do this... I know better because I'm a teacher! If only this didn't happen, then I would have been able to..."

"I should be able to..."

"I should..."

"I can't."

I crashed.

But this wasn't the first time I felt like I should be better than where I was. Even from my earliest days of teaching, I set the bar high. I needed to be the best, and nothing else would suffice.

Since the start of my career, I had a drive to be #1. During my district's budget crisis of 2011, when others delayed applying elsewhere, I knew right away I had to start looking for another job. I didn't want to wait to officially be put on the furlough list. I was in my third year teaching, right at the cutoff between who got to stay and who had to go. It didn't feel fair. Not to mention, that Fall semester, I began my Master's program. At the start of that year, I felt connected to my school and my colleagues and had such hope and gratitude for my development. I was in a good place. On top of that, I was doing all of the things you were supposed to do:

1. Find a job.
2. Teach
3. Obtain more credentials.
4. Become a master teacher.

At that time, I was on Step 3, but Step 4 has been the carrot I've been chasing my whole career.

Before the furlough news hit the district, I was gleefully pressing on with my Master's studies. I wanted to learn as much as possible about literacy instruction, a passion that still lives within me today. While it wasn't the best working full-time during the day and then having to still do homework at night, it was surprisingly easier to manage than I thought. And the coursework itself felt right up my alley.

The first time I heard about the Teachers College Reading and Writing Project (TCRWP) at Columbia University, I knew I wanted to be a part of it. I devoured every word of Kathy Collins' *Growing Readers* text, a required reading for one of my courses.[16] I loved every time she referred to the schools as P.S. 205 or P.S. 91. It was so giant. It was so much bigger than me. When my boss and principal at the time lent me her *Units of Study* for Writing Workshop, created by Lucy Calkins and her colleagues at TCRWP, I felt like I'd gone to heaven.[17] I felt so full of gratitude for being seen. I thought my boss could be my mentor and that I was on my way to being her mentee.

Reading Collins' and Calkin's words about literacy instruction filled my soul. It felt exactly the way I had hoped to grow my practice. It became the bar that I held above my head. THIS was how it should be done.*[18]

Step 4 felt like my absolute responsibility and goal as a teacher. If I wasn't working to become a master teacher, then what was I doing? Thus, I kept trying to achieve and get closer to what I thought "master teachers" did.

I believed Master Teachers were organized, kept good records, and built a kind and caring rapport with their students. With my propensity towards literacy development, they held an extreme knowledge base around reading instruction, both in understanding and execution. But it wasn't just language arts they paid attention to; they showed care and time to all subjects. Every curriculum was waiting to be melded into something more. And for extra credit, the icing on the cake, the all-star teacher firmly and easily managed her class. She had a stellar rapport with students and their families, and *other* teachers knew she was good, too.

By all means, these *are* qualities of a great educator, but what I failed to see was to what end. I did not give myself markers to assess my progress; therefore, I always felt behind. I always felt like I was chasing, aiming, and reaching for the next thing. The next thing—the thing that would make me a master teacher—kept getting further and further out of reach. Whether that was because of district furloughs or negativity in the workplace, my next achievement constantly felt like something both out of my control and in it. Only, I hadn't managed to figure out how to truly accomplish it. On top of that, because of the expectations I put on myself to achieve 100% success with every student, I failed to see the real-life barriers and challenges before me.

One of the hardest things for me is thinking that because I learned something, I won't have a problem again. I believe that because I know the material, I *should be able to* enact it. Whenever, wherever. I should just be able to dial it up. And especially, "because I'm a teacher." Because I know better.

That's where I found myself in 2013, 2018, and again starting in 2020. I was caught up in my own personal hell. I couldn't see a way out. There wasn't a way out, at least no easy trick door to escape from. I was in it. The Thick. Foggy. Heavy. Crushing defeat of my reality. The burnout was real.

"This is not at all how I pictured my life to be," I thought on repeat.

And why should it? I had so much good lined up, especially once the school year ended in 2019.

It finally came to me as we awaited our Visa approvals to move to Canada; the book idea I'd been waiting for! This book was going to change the world! I could finally put into words the uncertainty I'd been holding about education. I knew the way forward. And it all started with me—with us. We would look at our behaviors and actions and go from conditioned responses to conscious awareness. This book was for the teachers, but ultimately for the children. It was a chance to give them a new life and change the status quo. This book, this work, reverberated with possibility. It all started with noticing the means and changing our responses, reactions, and mindsets about how we view childhood expectations, particularly at school and home.

During the 2018-2019 school year, after resigning from my position at Montessori School of Oakland and taking the part-time position at a private school, I was lighter.

With school behind me and summer ahead, I felt ready and refreshed to give this book the space to be born. This was my next "career move." I could feel it.

I started waking early before my children, banking on the fact they were predictable sleepers. I began my "me time" mornings: coffee and journal, coffee and journal. Each morning, I began a reflection and intention practice. Soon, the words started to flow.

I felt on top of the world.

When we planned our move to Canada, I felt a high like no other. I had spontaneously stopped drinking, and for the six months prior, I was building good habits atop good habits. I regained presence and awareness and was genuinely content with work and home life. All my buckets were full, as I liked to say. I deleted social media, went to bed by 9 pm, had the luxury of house cleaners (which, by the way, is not bougie, contrary to what I first thought. This was a lifesaver!), and was generally rocking at life. I couldn't wait to move to Canada and start something new. To keep this good thing going.

I was so excited to have the opportunity to be home with my girls, and for the first time in my life, I wasn't worried or concerned about my work. I trusted where I was. It would all work out, I believed.

And then things began to stall.

At first, it was because I told myself this idea was too good to keep to myself. That it's probably incredibly self-indulgent and entitled to believe that I could do this thing—write a book—on my own. And, spoiler alert. It was. That book never got written. But it's not because I couldn't do it. It's because I thought I couldn't do it. It's because my *inner saboteur* got in the way.*[19]

My entire internal world started to shake. Soon, I felt like a fraud, a foe, an imposter. I started to doubt myself. I tried to ignore it and focus on the positives—I had this *brilliant* book idea—but that only took me so far.

Not long after, just when I got used to the moves and found a rhythm, the song changed. Events around me became out of my control. This pushed the book idea further out of reach, which also meant it drove a wedge between me and education.

Then, especially in 2020, I wasn't sure I should even be using my voice. Or when and where to use it. Not to mention, I could barely put into practice what I wanted to preach. I wasn't sure what to hold on to anymore. I flopped. And believed it was all my fault.

And because I couldn't admit I was struggling, there was no way for me to see any grace in my mistakes. I didn't think I should be making mistakes! I was expecting to do this work perfectly because I knew better.

During my struggles, rather than face my own inadequacy or shortcomings (which is really to say, what makes me a human being), I dove deeper into what it would mean to find perfection. Yet the chase of trying to capture *more* made me feel *less than*. It's like the further I reached, the more my confidence eroded.

Which made it all the more confusing.

In the classroom, I always felt confident about my belief in "choices within limits," but suddenly, in 2019, it felt like everything I was doing at home was with a hammer. My intention to provide structure was met with my internal blarehorn of "STOP TRYING TO CONTROL YOUR KIDS, CHRISTINA. STOP TRYING TO CONTROL." I didn't know where I stood anymore.

At the start of my stay-at-home venture, I couldn't see that the structure and order I discarded—the foundation that served me so well during my teaching days—left me puzzled, confused, and on crumbling ground. I couldn't connect the feeling of spinning in my head with the fact that I flipped my life upside down. I found myself in uncharted waters.

And because we decided to withdraw our children from their upcoming preschool after COVID-19 hit, we decided that I would attempt to homeschool them. After all, I was a teacher. After all, I have my Montessori training. After all, I *should* be able to do this.

It went exactly as you could imagine for a high-functioning, anxiety-ridden perfectionist who doesn't realize she's depressed and is dealing with both collective and individual grief. It felt like an absolute failure. And whatever limit I thought I had reached before, this was a whole new low.

I constantly questioned held beliefs in pursuit of something better out of fear that what I was doing wasn't good or right. I can see now that I went too far. I wouldn't go so far as to say my questioning wasn't *necessary*—it did get me here, after all. But it does feel like the equivalent of going around the whole block when I could have just reversed a little. Maybe I didn't need to change everything all at once. But that's only something I can say now.

I wasn't sure how to be a Teacher vs. Mama when it came down to it. The training I'd relied on and felt successful within the classroom felt wrong in the confines of our home. Not to mention, I still had yet to fully figure out my new educational philosophy other than a desire to change the areas where I sought control, which, *hello*, was everywhere.

Trying to change my approach and not wanting to "fall back" on what had worked in the past threw me for a loop. I couldn't find my footing. And then, being a twin parent, I saw how incredibly different my children were as it related to this new venture. What worked for one didn't work for the other. For the one who presented as liking school, things were fine. However, my other daughter, who was only three years old then, immediately rejected the idea of school.

Her reaction of trying to hide in the corner didn't feel personal, but it still stung. It made me think back to previous students of mine and how I glossed over some of their beginning-of-the-year fears. Now, I could see them all with so much more understanding. I wanted to call the whole thing off right there and scoop her into my arms.

On top of homeschooling, fueled by the general anxiety of living through the pandemic and deeply desiring to correct social injustice, every day felt like a fight. The bricks of expectation I put on myself to change the world, both at home and at large, weighed me down. Not to mention, to do so with a completely new, still under-revision, playbook. A playbook

that, if only I could actually get a minute to work on, I'd figure out. Tough plays to achieve for a stay-at-home parent with
zero time to self *and* quarantined. Any breaks I did get felt
more like being in the penalty box. How do you change the
world in two-minute increments?

It never felt like I was doing enough. I felt like it was all up
to me because "I knew better." *Should know better.* And, before
I knew it, I was bitter, angry, and ashamed. I felt I shouldn't
be so challenged because this was my area of expertise. So,
when I struggled, I was embarrassed and resentful. I was angry
at myself for questioning my beliefs and approaches and not
having the ability to bring them to fruition. This was my "Step
4," continuing to play out at home.

I desperately wanted to forge a new path between the present and how I saw the future, but I kept running into dead
ends.

When I tried, I felt wrong. When I didn't try, I felt wrong.
Nothing made me feel good. I cried every day for two months
and never once thought there might be more going on. I only
called it depression before because it's something I can name
now. At the time, this was just another Wednesday, my new
normal.

During this time, it was difficult to determine who was "failing" more: mom-me or teacher-me. And who's supposed to
know better than *Mom*? Than *teacher*? Truthfully, I felt hit
twice.

I couldn't exactly see it at the time, but it was very remi-
niscent of my feelings when I returned to the classroom after
my maternity leave.

As my girls were nearing their first birthday and my school
year was wrapping up, I knew I had to seek help. I stood out-

side my school building on a balmy afternoon as I waited for a staff meeting to begin and called my health provider. I had to at least inquire again if maybe I actually did have postpartum depression. I kicked up dust as I paced in the parking lot. *What will I say when they answer?* I still felt nervous to claim the words "postpartum depression," but the urgency with which they were received gave me hope. An appointment with an intake counselor was scheduled for that same week.

It's what I had expected to happen when I first mentioned this concern.

At my six-week checkup, I brought up my worries to my OB doctor, but I was quickly dismissed. "It just sounds like you need to give yourself a break. You have twins," she said.

This dismissal of my health both stunned and relieved me. I felt relieved I didn't "have" postpartum depression because, on the surface, it gave me the clear that there wasn't something "wrong" with me. PPD was something *you* could have, and that was OK, but it wasn't something *I* would let happen (remember that one?).*20 Additionally, I've since learned about postpartum and perinatal *anxiety*, which would have explained so much had I been operating under that awareness and had a professional notice.

And this is why when my doctor dismissed me, I felt in limbo. I was in the clear, but not really. Because while I may not have had this *label*, I still felt its presence. It made it very difficult for me to trust my feelings and seek adequate care. On one hand, I leaned into being grateful for what I did have: two beautiful, healthy children and a loving, supportive partner. On the other hand, I had an entire profile of grief, anger, resentment, bitterness, and anxiety that was being kept at bay.

After that appointment, I pushed it all into my filing cabinet. Or so I thought.

Reeling from the most difficult school year to date and feeling like both a failure at home and work, that new intake counselor no sooner sat me down when the tears started flowing. I explained my situation and story. I went through the miscarriage, the surprise of twins, the grief during childbirth, the aftermath and family drama, the lack of familial proximity, the feeling that because I was a teacher, I thought I could handle all that came with parenthood, the ridiculous, grueling school year where I went back to full-time teaching when my twins were only four-month-old babies and had my public breakdown. I also talked about the constant fear I had that my children would die. In all this, I stated, I just wasn't doing enough. Not enough to get them the right toys, the right clothes, the right environment, the right foods, the right childcare.

I continued to dump out the contents of my purse: At school, my inner critic told me I wasn't prepared enough. I didn't care enough. I wasn't handling classroom management well. I was a shell pretending to be a superhero. I went through my days as a hollowed human, hoping that no one would notice how badly I was failing. I felt genuine pride as a parent for completing the maternal checklist: feed, pump, sleep, repeat. I thought my worth and evaluation as a parent came from successfully keeping my kids from being hungry, tired, or irritable. If I could do these things and control them, I would be a successful caregiver.

Joy was filling my phone with 10,000 pictures of my kids, but beyond that, I didn't feel much besides tiredness and an ongoing ache for things to be better, different.

Is this normal? Is this how motherhood is supposed to feel? Why does it feel like I'm always wrong? I exposed my deepest fears to her.

When I reached the end of telling my story to the counselor, she nodded and paused. I was sure she was going to confirm my fears of postpartum depression. Instead, she said something I couldn't believe—something I would have never predicted.

She said I was dealing with perfectionism.

Was she not listening to what I was saying? I am not a perfectionist! I don't need everything to be perfect and clean and just right. My mind went to images of my coworker's pristine shelves and to mine collecting dust as I sat there.

Perfectionism certainly didn't pertain to me! But all that came out was, "Huh?! How so?"

She detailed how I wasn't recognizing how difficult my situation really was, and because of this, I was giving myself no room to breathe. No room to fault. No room to say, "This is hard." Because I felt I should do it all, I wasn't talking to myself kindly when I made mistakes. I didn't reach out to others for help, so I felt alone and isolated when I stumbled. And ruminating over unproductive thoughts—regrets or fears—kept me in a state of never feeling like enough. There was always something on my plate for me to do, but I was never satisfied with the outcome.

This explanation started to land.

It was then that she introduced me to the work of Dr. Kristen Neff, a leading researcher on self-compassion. Dr. Neff is currently an associate professor of educational psychology at the University of Texas at Austin. For nearly twenty years, she's been educating others on how to live with more compassion. She believes self-compassion has three parts: self-kindness, shared humanity, and mindfulness.[21]

Still, at the time, I wasn't convinced.

I thought back to my coworker's immaculate and orderly classroom, to the images of people needing things to be "just right" for them to proceed. "Yeah, this doesn't sound like me," I thought.

The counselor explained more about Dr. Neff's research and guiding principles. She shared that when we're gentle to ourselves in the face of our imperfections when we understand that we are not the only ones struggling or feeling the way we do, and when we practice presence over letting our thoughts and feelings run wild, we can come to hold ourselves with more care and comfort. We can begin to build the muscles of self-compassion. At its core, self-compassion is the comfort and care you give yourself when you're going through a hard time. It includes the same level of tenderness and nurturing you'd give to a friend in need.

In shame, we crumble, and in love, we grow. And this was the first moment, of many, that led me to a new path of embracing who I am, mistakes and all. Of course, this was before the hurts of 2020 piled up. Yet, what I learned since then, outside the classroom, transformed how I see our work in it.

I see now that for as much as I believe many of us carry the weight of our own perfectionist tendencies (which can be a strength), there is much more at play than we thought.

Let's have a look.

Dr. Sophie Brock, a current Motherhood Studies Sociologist, has identified and named an invisible force that mothers and non-mothers alike contend with. She calls this the "perfect mom myth."[22] This encompasses where that "do it all" mindset originates. Because of the similarities of working with children and youth and the overlap in expectations for mothers and teachers, I've extended that term also to see it as the "perfect teacher myth."

If you're not a parent, you may wonder how this applies to you. I include a parenting perspective because we *are* in the people and family business. We work with children and youth. Our students' well-being is directly tied to how their family is cared for, including but not limited to the systemic barriers that impact them. *Your* ability to provide for *your* class and *your* family is directly tied to the health care, finances, and social services you receive. When we live in a system that does not financially support healthcare and childcare, we are left with a nation of people who feel like they're failing. And by many standards, they are because they don't have what they need. In short, if we do not take care of the mother, the family suffers.

Yet, here's where the disconnect lies. I recognize now that when I was in the classroom, and as a pre-service teacher, I couldn't accurately identify the systems we were up against. I couldn't see what I was facing, whether that was gender inequality, racial inequity, economic injustice, the lack of maternal care, or the trauma that can come from such living conditions.

Instead, I saw the exhaustion. I saw the poverty. I saw which parents showed up to conferences and which children were sent to the office. I saw students below grade level.

I didn't see my own bias or realize the impact my own expectations had on the reality in front of me. Instead, I saw "failure" all around.

As Dr. Sophie Brock says, I internalized external systems. Rather than looking at something else as "being the problem" or even having the awareness that outside forces were impacting how I saw myself, I became the problem.

Move over, Beyoncé. Taylor's here now. It was me.

I didn't see how I had an incomplete picture of why or how those circumstances existed. I saw my work. I saw my job. And I believed that as an educator, I was to achieve at all costs. I assumed it was my responsibility to help kids overcome everything, despite what was thrown against them, against us. Moreover, if families were struggling, my bias and ignorance suggested it was because of their ineptitude or lack of maintaining responsibilities—an area I seriously misjudged.

I felt relieved when I learned about the "Perfect Mother Myth," discussed by Dr. Sophie Brock and *Momwell* founder and therapist Erica Djossa. I immediately felt seen for my struggles, and more importantly, I didn't feel alone.

The Perfect Mother Myth is devised as *musts* and *shoulds* and internalized expectations for how we view "mothers, mothering, and motherhood" to be. In other words, what we perceive it looks like and feels like to be a mom. While that will look different for each person, we all have been birthed into a world holding these expectations, regardless of whether we are a parent. Unless we stop to analyze these long-held beliefs, we often unknowingly participate. The myth perpetuates because it sneaks around our subconscious.

What's more, the myth gets passed on without our awareness. Then, it outlives us. And while it can and does change from generation to generation, it is at the mercy of those who abide by it. Which, unfortunately, is most of us, daresay all of us. Even if we are not moms. Brock and Djossa say, "It's the water we swim in."

The waters that propel us to *Do as much as we can without breaking.* And *you had better look pretty, too (coordination helps). I'm only a good mom if I do this. I must be a bad mom if I do that. I can't let anyone down, no less my children.* And probably, the cincher is *I must always enjoy motherhood (especially because it was my choice to become a parent).*

When our actual experiences don't match this, we don't blame motherhood; we blame ourselves. Moreover, we look towards the other moms who seem to have it all together, making us feel even more at a loss. *What do they have that I don't? Why is this easier for them? I didn't think this was going to be so hard. Why is this so hard? I must be failing...*

Often, we don't realize these overarching frameworks around mothering have been present since childhood. We don't realize our beliefs about our mothers, aunts, grandmothers, neighbors, and women at large, especially as portrayed in the media, until we find ourselves butting up against what we can't do. Or what we expect them to do.

Only when our lived experiences don't match our expectations do we stop. And in that pause, two things can happen: We either recognize that we've been putting such heavy expectations on ourselves and adjust accordingly. Or, we keep going. It's the latter that typically happens. We put our heads down, droop our shoulders even more, and believe we are singularly failing. There's something wrong with us because we don't have the most behaved children, the perfectly coordinated outfits, or our joy doesn't match what we see in others' pictures. We don't stop to consider, maybe it is something more.

What turns the myth on its head is when we shine a light on it. When we look closer at these aspects of our mother self, our mothering actions, or our collective motherhood experience, we see that something doesn't feel right. We begin to notice that the words we've used to describe ourselves, i.e., "good mom," "bad mom," and the way we measure our merit, e.g., how much we love our children or by how much we do for them, is the way it's always been done, not the way it *must* be done. Moreover, we recognize those "this or that" terms can't possibly cover the breadth and depth of human beings raising other human beings. And on top of that, we recognize the words we're using to describe ourselves are causing harm, whether we can see it or not: self-directed hate towards ourselves and daggers towards others.

We can't fix what we don't see.

When we break from the pressures and expectations that have been mounting against us, the ones that whisper, "*Achieve Perfection*," this status quo of motherhood can never make it to shore. Conversely, if we never examine these notions and are prone to letting criticism and judgment seep in, we are a tidal wave waiting to happen.

But that is what's shifting. Partly in thanks to Dr. Brock and Erica Djossa, among countless other maternal health advocates. That perfect "way" of motherhood doesn't work. And never has. We're starting to see that the facade we've been putting up can come down. When we do this, we begin living in the *Land of And*. And just as importantly, it brings awareness to what's been imperceptible up to this point.

When we internalize external factors, such as culture and social conditioning, and then face struggle or burnout, we have difficulty understanding why. That was certainly my experience. That is what makes the Motherhood Myth so potent: No one can see it.

At least, not until you train your eye to spot it.

And what I see now is how this also carries over to education.

When I first started using the word "Teacherhood," it was because I knew we needed a term to more accurately cover the experience of being a teacher—our individual backgrounds and our collective offerings.

Teacherhood differs from being "the teacher" or even the act of teaching itself. Related terms like mother and motherhood inspire it. However, I was surprised to learn that the differences in those words also make up the Perfect Mother Myth. In that case, it looks at the mother, the mothering, and the motherhood experience as three related but unique entities. Unsurprising, however, is how much I relate this to education and why I believe there's also a Perfect Teacher Myth.

And for that, we're returning to one of the earliest education reformers, Catherine Beecher, the poster child for making today's teaching force what it is.

Two hundred years ago, a shift occurred, and women were told they were innately more suited to teaching than men. These middle-class White women were upheld to the vision of Beecher and her counterpart Horace Mann, who believed in their angelic, pristine qualities to carry over to teaching.

This became the standard because this became the model—and the bar to which teachers were held. Soon, with the operation of Normal Schools preparing a new teaching force of prim and "morally superior" women, while men departed schools in the dozens, candidates became groomed to fit this made-up model. What was first described as their natural penchant and demeanor towards making capable, nurturing educators became what was sought.

So now the question becomes: If you don't fit this model, is something wrong with you? Are you unfit to teach? Are you lacking critical components of what makes a great educator? (And, *what if you don't even really want to become a teacher, but this is the lane you're told to stay in?* Maybe that will be in my someday-to-be-published-Education anthology, too.)

Let's also add the fact that Beecher and Mann did not pave the way for *all* women; only White, middle-class women were viewed as educational pioneers. Simply put, women of color were not given their due chance. Not to mention the ramifications of *Brown v. Board of Education*, along with the currents of institutionalized racism, pushed out successful Black educators from the field—effects that we're still feeling today (Education anthology, for sure).[24]

So, how does this relate to the "perfect teacher?"

Since the start of formal education, teachers have always been seen as agents of social change. It's been our job to lift the individual so we can lift society. So, if we fail—*if we're not perfect*—everyone fails. Our society goes down, too.

The fate of America has been in our hands. At least, that is the message we hear. And while you and I, and generations of teachers, have carried that expectation with honor, we never stopped to say, "This is too heavy."

Instead, over time, to ensure we didn't fail, we worked harder, better, and more perfectly. We told ourselves we must be successful and make no mistakes. Remember, a good teacher does *this*. And a bad teacher does *that*.

A list of musts and shoulds...

A mountain of pressure was placed on our backs. And today, we're ready to say, "This is too much to carry."

It's important for you, for me, for all the teachers who read this to recognize this weight we've been carrying because the struggle becomes personal if you feel you don't fit the mold. *The perfect teacher who can do it all.* If you can't carry the weight, clearly, it's you. You're not strong enough. It couldn't ever be the systems and forces against you.

Whether in the 1800s or today, when we hold anyone to a higher standard than the support we give them or eliminate their access to success, they will crumble. If we put them on a pedestal, that becomes a glorified stage for abuse; they're prone to the stones from the viewing party. Everyone can see what they're doing and has an opinion, but no one is willing to help. The sticks and stones break bones, but the names also hurt us.

Because if we're not, if we're not that version of the "perfect teacher" that so many make us out to be, then we're labeled as "bad" or "failing." And worse, we're the ones who usually do the name-calling. At least, I know I was.

But what if there were a new model? What if we could change how we view the perfect teacher? What if we start by acknowledging there is no perfect teacher?

Of course, there *are* knowledge, skills, and dispositions that make for an effective teacher. I'm not denying that. And, of course, I'm not arguing for toxic teachers to stay in the game. But what if we could make room for multiple versions of a good teacher?

There is no one way.

But that takes radical awareness and courage to make the shifts we want to see.

What's inside comes out, and what's outside comes in. In the next chapter, we'll peel back another layer to see where our insecurities have been hiding, providing another way for you to see yourself and your struggles in a new light. I'm ready. Are you?

Consider This:
- Which areas of your life do you seek perfection?
- How have you unknowingly participated in the "Perfect Teacher Myth?" Where could you lower the bar for the expectations you hold for yourself?

5

It's OK to Make Mistakes

You are stronger than your scariest thoughts.

Now that we've looked at two myths that have lived rent-free in our subconscious, I want to address what happens when those beliefs collide—when they team up and become supervillains. For people like you and me, who are not only inundated with the constant stream of external pressures but also live in the waters of our own internal drive for perfection, this supervillain pushes us to the edge.

For me, colliding identities in motherhood and teacherhood over the past couple of years created the perfect storm: the tsunami of doubt and overwhelm. I want to showcase, again, what that looks like when we're unaware of what we're dealing with. In later chapters, we will look at how we can use our perfectionism to our advantage (believe it or not, it can be a good thing, too!), but for now, let's dive back into what it looks like and feels like when we're treading water.

I don't know about you, but my inner critic likes to put on a bit of a show. Throughout my career, and during times of stress, my inner critic comes out to dance. She tips and taps her way around my prefrontal cortex and shuffles away any logic, leaving me with a show-stopping soloist who won't give anyone else the mic. She demands the spotlight. And my tender heart is sitting on the velvety cushions of the theater, stunned, an audience of one.

For all the dramatics and work that my inner critic does to take the stage, you would think she'd want recognition, but she doesn't. She only ever wants me. And I can't seem to take my eyes off of her.

If I get up to leave, she threatens to burn the whole place down.

Does yours sound like that, too? RuPaul likes to call this our "inner saboteur."

As teachers, we're taught the relationship we have with our students is paramount, the relationship we have with their families is crucial, but no word is mentioned about the relationship we have with ourselves. It is the foundation for it all.

Although I held myself up highly in private as a child, I always felt a nagging presence that I wasn't enough. That it wasn't real because it's not what I showed up as—that this part of me was just pretending. Especially the parts of me who made worlds with Barbies and imagined wild futures in dance and music compilations. Who wrote stories and searched for solutions for interpersonal relationships and fix-it projects around the house. And later, who, one day, could be *Teacher-of-the-Year*—the adult version of the honor roll.

I had big dreams for my life. It was teaching that finally gave me the identity I'd been restless to find. I knew what I could do, *if only I could get out of my skin or away from the people who I perceived were in my way.* And I've learned how often I have been in my own way.

Can I share an embarrassing story?

Early in my career, when I perceived that another person was taking my limelight, my inadequacies and fears of not belonging rang louder than a fire drill.

I stood in my classroom next to the windows and side exit. Outside, snow was still on the ground. I overheard some muffled adult voices coming from the adjoining classroom. Their laughter pierced my heart. Surely, they were talking about me. Why else would they be quiet? These weren't people with quiet voices!

With my heart thumping, I entered the room. "Just say it out loud," I blurted. The three of them, my grade-level colleagues, looked up, confused. "Yeah, I know you were saying something about me," I continued.

"Huh? Nooo. Christina, we were—" I saw her lips still moving, but I couldn't hear her words. I froze.

My god, what an idiot! Why did I say something? And in such a confrontational way?! I thought.

"Sorry," I mumbled. "I just thought... it just seemed like you were saying something about me." My voice trailed off. "I'm sorry... I had a bad day."

Thankfully, they forgave my imposition. But days later, my body still swelled with embarrassment and jealousy. She, my friend—the new teacher—was getting all the attention. *Of course she's better than me. I suck. Of course they like her better than me.*

This was my second year teaching and the first time I felt a pang of envy for a colleague. Until this point, I felt like an all-star, and now someone else was getting my starting position. *Maybe I'm not as great as I thought.* My inner child wept in the corner.

Over a decade later, I'm still not sure what makes me feel more ashamed: the fact I accused my coworkers or that I felt so little of my worth in that moment. Maybe I don't need to choose. Either way, I was caught up in my own head.

She's better than me.
I messed it all up.
They're talking about me. I just know it.
I'm not a good teacher.
I can't believe I did that. I know better.
I should have done better. I know better.
I could have done better. I know better.
Why does this always happen?

You know these thoughts. The ones that run rampant in your head all day. On the nonstop train of confusion, doubt, and inner sabotage. Always coming back to collect more. Maybe for some, the thoughts go by like the clouds. Here, and then there. But for me, for us, it's like each one gets stuck in the frame. Thoughts stuck on moments stuck on thoughts. And before I know it, it's a ten-car pile-up in my head. Past, present, and future are all smashed together.

Why *does* this always happen?

Thankfully, I found that answer in the form of therapy.

A few years after the incident above, after leaving my position at Erie Montessori School to return to my previous district in 2013, I was seizing with regret again. I choose to go back for financial gain and the hope of inserting some Montessori philosophy into a traditional setting. Yet, nothing was going according to plan. Every day was a struggle. Within three days of taking on the new assignment, a parent called me "harsh." And maybe I was. I was angry and confused and not the best version of myself. On top of work challenges, my interpersonal relationships were suffering. My husband tried to be supportive but felt drained from my constant low moods. I felt alone and burned.

Reeling from the garbage fire of my career and life decisions, I desperately needed guidance to help me navigate the guilt, shame, and regret of my choices in the classroom and at home. At that point in my life, I felt like a failure at every turn. So I did the very thing I was so afraid to do but desperately sought: therapy.

It was a scary first step, but a much-needed one.

On Wednesday evenings, I'd drive to the therapist's office, which shared a building with a vacuum center. I'd walk the small staircase to the basement floor and sit in the same green cushioned lobby chair while waiting my turn. I'd stare at the brightly colored fish tank, a sharp and mesmerizing contrast to the dim lighting in the room. When the session before me ended, I'd enter the room, not much bigger than a closet, sit down in the oversized recliner, and take a breath.

Usually, a forced breath. Usually, a breath out of necessity from holding in all the ones before it. I'd try to look around the room to relax, my feet or fingers tapping their nearest surfaces. The therapist, however, was patient and calm. When ready, I'd begin with what was on my mind.

I did that every week for six months until I moved out of Pennsylvania. Not every session felt like a win, and still, to this day, I use that first experience as a marker to tell if the therapist and I are a good fit. But for all that I still had yet to learn, it gave me so much more. It gave me a new perspective. A new way to see life. A complete 180.

I was expecting to go to therapy to better learn how to take care of my mounting regrets, but I walked away with so much more.

My first therapist introduced me to "cognitive distortions," or thinking patterns that tend to cause us to view situations, ourselves, and our future with negativity and subjective lenses. About one month into our sessions, I walked in as I did any other week but left completely changed. At 27 years old, with half a decade in the classroom, I walked away from that appointment with a phrase I'll never forget: Thoughts are not facts. Yes, I'll say that again! Yes, louder and in all caps!

THOUGHTS ARE NOT FACTS.

Thoughts are not facts. It was mind-blowing. It was inconceivable. It was freedom. I felt like I was entering a new reality. And for all intents and purposes, I was.

I know this because if hating myself was a sport, I'd have won the top trophy. Some of my earliest memories are of wishing I were different. Wishing my teeth were straighter, my legs longer, and my hair curly. I wished I could bend and contort like all my favorite gymnasts instead of being the stiff board I really was. In soccer, I relied on my speed, which always made me feel like a standout, but as I reached the Varsity level, I realized I didn't have the footwork to keep up with my teammates. I realized I wasn't all that fast—at least not for track's 100-meter dash. My confidence plummeted.

As I got older, my dislikes turned from outward to inward. I hated my shyness, the way I'd close up around any boy or adult, the way I hated making eye contact, and the way my throat constricted whenever I wanted to stand up for myself. I hated that I knew I had a well of love, spirit, and spunk in me, but I didn't know how to express that. I was too afraid to express that.

Soon, I toggled between disliking what I saw on the outside and being discouraged by my feeling of lack inside. Middle school Christina turned into high school Christina turned into college Christina… young woman, teacher, mother… all carrying these same bags of self-hatred.

Only, I didn't realize it was even self-hatred. If you would have asked me if I hated myself, I would have said no. That I had much to love, and that's what's so tricky about our self-image. We hold ourselves up highly and slam ourselves to the ground in the same motion. We pick and prod and trim and tweeze, bemoaning our ugly bits and dismissing ourselves for not being perfect.

We keep an ideal in our heads of what we and our life is supposed to look like. Formed from years of social conditioning and unconscious absorption, we don't realize the harm we do to ourselves *because this is how it's always been.* For as long as we can remember, we've always had the loud critic telling us we should be a different way.

Leaner

Taller

Fitter

Smarter

Prettier

Funnier

More loving

More courageous

More palatable

Less moody

Less irritable

Less abrasive

Less *us.*

We leave childhood with invisible scars of not being good enough. And this isn't our parents, families, or friends' fault. We are all swimming in the sea of inadequacy. This is the world we live in.

But there's hope. Thank God, there's hope. You being here today, reading this book, is hope. Hope exists because change is always possible. But you can't hate your way into changing. It has to come from a place of love, deep love.

So, how do we do it? How do we begin to love ourselves a little bit more? It starts by recognizing where we've been. Personally, I uncovered how much-hidden hate existed by looking at my old journals.

I've always been an avid journaler, dating back to my freshman year in high school. Then, I needed an outlet to process my teenage rage and angst. Now, well, it's the same.

All these years later, journaling has remained a godsend to me. It's taken on different forms, from cataloging my day to being a confidant to helping me ask myself difficult questions, allowing me space to write freely and creatively, and witnessing my spiritual development.

Over 20 years, I have accumulated *a lot*. Then, notebooks would span about two years, but now I can barely go two months before filling the pages. I recently suggested to my husband that we should buy a safe—not to protect legal documents, but to house my notebooks! They are a treasure and a story in and of themselves. From my overly circular cursive penmanship in my teenage years to indecipherable strokes written at full speed during my roaring 20s, they are who I am.

One of the greatest gifts journaling has given me is a window into myself. I keep my journals not only for prosperity but for research. Unintentionally, I've given myself a way to see my mind, particularly at difficult periods of my life.

A few years ago, after thinking about a high school break-up, I pulled out that very first journal. Interested in remembering the details of that event, I was shocked by what I read. Not that anything was different about that breakup; I still recalled the anguish and anger I felt then, but I couldn't believe how mean everyone was. The AOL Instant Messenger (AIM) conversations I printed between myself and my ex and his friends brought tears to my eyes. *Fifteen-year-old Christina didn't deserve to be spoken to that way.* My heart ached for my teenage self. I wanted to jump into the pages and wrap her in my arms. I wanted to tell her everything that young girls need to hear.

Once I got over that surprise hurt, I was disturbed by what I continued to read. *I* was so mean *to myself.* From body image put-downs to general slams over my "stupidity," I couldn't believe what I was reading. I couldn't believe this is how I spoke to myself. I couldn't believe I couldn't remember this was how I talked to myself. I returned downstairs to the basement and pulled out the journal from 2013, a time of deep personal and professional hurt. Again. This demeaning, albeit pain-filled, voice spread across the lines. I realized I couldn't remember the bully's voice because this is how I talked to myself on the daily. This was still happening. I vowed to change the way I spoke to myself, particularly in my writing.

It took conscious effort to write in this new way, but I was already starting to see how much more cared-for I felt by myself. This new form of journaling was helping to transform my self-image. I went from someone who constantly wrote about my mishaps with disdain to a person who cataloged them with compassion. More than that, speaking to myself with pause and purpose opened up an even more unexpected discovery: That I could be a person who makes change.

The voice in our head, especially when we make mistakes, is so indistinguishable we barely notice it. It's who we are, we say. And that voice has been with us our whole life. Writing has allowed me to see how to get out of my way. It's helped me see my conditioned beliefs about myself, whether absorbed unconsciously through societal messages or how I spoke to myself.

When we allow ourselves to see ourselves and our habits honestly and with compassion, we open the door to a new way of living.

In 2019, about two weeks into our move to Canada, my journaling evolved again. Perhaps due to my isolation and loneliness of not having a nearby confidant and colliding with all the emotion bubbling from being around my family and away from my husband, I realized that I needed to be my own cheerleader. I needed a new voice to soothe me when everything was going wrong. Enter my *Self-Compassion and Grace Journal*. A little red-woven bullet notebook gifted by my friend that I decided would serve a unique purpose.

Instead of talking to my journal, my journal spoke to me. I wrote the words I needed to hear. This voice, part friend, part mentor, was warm, caring, and emphatically pro-Christina. She knew my heart, and she could see my pain. But she wouldn't let me live in worry. She wouldn't let me stay in pity. She was there for me. And in turn, I became there for myself.

It was another life-changing journal moment for me. Over the last couple of years of becoming more aware of the critical voice I was using towards myself and vowing to speak more positively, worry still flooded the pages. Writing about the emotions overwhelming me helped me to dump and process what was swirling around my mind, but often, I'd be left with a sense of restlessness. I still felt panged by whatever was consuming me. It still tugged on me with urgency.

This voice was different. I found solace after writing, as if a friend were truly next to me. My best friends were miles and borders away. Sure, they were accessible by text, but that felt like too much energy at times. This journal was immediate. This was straightforward. This was me finding a way towards myself.

I became softer in those moments. The writing was smoothing out my edges and molding me into something new. Something I hadn't seen before. A more self-compassionate being. It also gave me hope. Relief. Whatever was consuming me wasn't going to be forever. This journal-friend could see that.

Sometimes, this voice would simply tell me, "It's OK. You've got this." Other times, she went deeper: *I can see how hard this is for you. This is a hard thing. And I know how upset you are that you lost your cool. It's going to be OK. I promise."*

Often, after hearing this gentle voice, my mind freed, and I became solution-oriented. Rather than stay panged with guilt or shame, I found a path forward. I gave myself the love and space I needed. I gave myself the self-compassion I craved.

This practice recalibrated the aftermath of my perceived mistakes and gave me grace and hope to do the next thing. To parent after remorse, to breathe after heartache.

In our low points, when it feels like we've messed up one too many times and regret coils its way around our neck, the Self-Compassion and Grace Journal is there to cut the tension. For me, this is most impactful when I need a "quick" pick-me-up when a friend is unavailable or may not have the words I'm seeking. I write as if that friend is right there next to me.

If Gandhi tells us to be the change we wish to see, this journal is a direct line to embodying that message. And it all started with a deep understanding that I needed to treat myself better. But I couldn't always see this so clearly. In fact, anytime anyone has ever told me "to go easy on myself," I often met their intended encouragement with slight disdain. *Didn't they know how hard this is to do? Maybe they just don't care like I do?*

While I believe there are many things at play, the truth is that "talking nicely to myself" has not come easy. In fact, my inner critic has been so strong my entire life that berating myself was just normal to me. I never thought to question it. That is until I started therapy and again when I happened upon my first journal from high school.

That's why, as high-striving individuals and educators who face constant demand and decision-making, it's crucial to be aware of our relationship with ourselves. And if I need to *SCREAM* this from the rooftops, I will because **S**elf-**C**ompassion **R**ules **E**verything **A**round **M**e.

Learning about self-compassion was like learning a new language. I truly had to pick new words to say to myself. It's where "talking to yourself like a friend" comes from. Learning about self-compassion, particularly Dr. Kristen Neff's research, allowed me to see that somewhere in my life, I inaccurately learned that life wasn't supposed to be complicated. At least not for me. At least not for hard workers. I believed that if I worked hard enough and did all the right things, then life would be easy—that I wouldn't struggle. Somewhere along my life, I learned I wasn't human. At least, I didn't understand what being human really meant. I didn't realize it was truly OK to make mistakes.

After the shock of the *perfectionism* label wore off from my postpartum appointment, I began to see areas of my life where

I had developed perfectionist behaviors. I looked back to the times in my teaching career when I applauded my reflection practices, but now, I saw the fear of failure underneath it all. I saw the nights I stayed up late to cut and glue and make materials precise. I saw how difficult it was to make mistakes or admit when I didn't know something because I didn't want to look new. I wanted to be the one who had it all together. I looked back to the nights I spent writing painstaking lessons, to the times I read and reread and read again an email I needed to send.

I also thought of an interview rejection I received where, afterwards, I lay gutted on my couch. Unmoveable, inconsolable—feeling and reeling from the regret of not doing a better job, of being denied. I thought back to my times of struggle when I couldn't figure out how to handle a challenging situation or when a child's behaviors felt beyond my skill set. I thought about how hard it was to confide in another coworker for fear that my image of a strong, knowledgeable teacher would be broken. I thought about the times I beat myself up for losing my cool, raising my voice, or showing some other undesirable emotion. I thought about all the times I feared my inadequacy.

And that's also what's tricky about perfectionism. It masks itself. I thought my behaviors and actions were friends helping me along. Helping me to be more responsible, more organized, more invested. And while it's true they *were* helping me in those endeavors, to a degree, they were also quietly, slowly, eating away at me. I couldn't see where I had crossed the line because the line kept moving. I couldn't see that I was my own worst enemy, holding myself to unrealistic expectations. And when I inevitably couldn't make everything around me work—or did so with the tightest grip possible—I blamed myself for all that went wrong. All the things I should have done. Could have done. Would have done. I thought about all the times I was angry and anguished I wouldn't get a second chance. That I was left with the outcome, whether I liked it or not. And let's be honest, I most often did *not* like it.

When I acknowledged that I was, in fact, a perfectionist, I could also see that self-compassion—in all the ways Dr. Neff's research outlines—was indeed the way forward. Yet, whether you identify with being a perfectionist or not, being able to treat yourself with kindness in the face of adversity has implications for us all.

In the six years since that postpartum appointment, I've also gone through many iterations of what perfectionism means, specifically, how society believes we should and shouldn't respond to "our perfectionism." Most importantly, I learned that self-compassion is the glue that holds us together. It rules everything around us.

Beyond *my* words, dear one, I hope you are finding the ones that allow kindness and compassion to stream into *your* system. That swirl in the waters of your being. That carry you out of self-judgment and into self-love.

I've spent enough years for the both of us, deluged in denial, criticism, and disappointment. I don't want you to stay there any longer.

We are not the sum of our mistakes.

And, there can always be change. But we must choose it.

Whether you journal or not, our words to ourselves have power. You will believe the things you tell yourself. Thankfully, we can rely on the self-compassion research by educators like Dr. Kristin Neff. We can see we deserve more kindness. We can recognize our shared humanity. We can see we're not alone.

When we pull up the bar on self-love and deeply believe we are worthy of repair, we grant ourselves the largest dose of freedom we've ever experienced. We become the miracle in an instant because—for that moment—we chose to see our world in a new way. And that is the beauty granted by allowing yourself to be human. When you understand that the *Making of Mistakes* is a path you can walk, you realize you don't need to be perfect to live well.

We've learned that, as crushing as making mistakes can feel, they don't break us forever. In fact, they often transform us into something new. Before I met Grace, I thought these mistakes disqualified me. I thought they showed my error and also my exit. I thought that making mistakes simply meant I wasn't good enough. It took me many years to learn that making mistakes is exactly how we grow.

Learning and relearning that we are works in process helps us grow grace in places we've let shrivel and dry. This primes our soul for our grief to permeate and replenish us. And it's OK if we don't know. The answers won't always be apparent. The way forward won't always be clear. But you are growing and molding and changing into the soft-hearted being you've always been meant to be. And the work is only getting started.

Consider This:
- How does knowing "thoughts are not facts" change your relationship to your inner chatter?
- Which mistakes feel the hardest? What would giving yourself grace sound like?

6

You Are
Learning, Too

*Each time you walk through this door
you get a fresh start.*

Incidents like the classroom scene portrayed in the last chapter were just one example of how I've been in my head throughout my life. Rather, how I've viewed my life because of what was going on in my head. In my defense, I didn't know what I was missing. I didn't realize thoughts aren't facts. I had to be taught that. From elementary to middle school and on to college and career, whatever was going on in my head, I believed it. This was me, after all.

Unfortunately, we get in the way of ourselves without ever realizing it. To those of us who struggle with obsessive thoughts or constant worry, this just feels like another day. This is our normal. But when you learn about your thought patterns and that you can and do have the ability to monitor your reactions to life's disappointments, annoyances, and letdowns, you realize you have more power than you know.

Of course, if held too tightly, it can also overpower you.

In short, we often overthink situations, downplay our successes, and dwell on our failures or mistakes. Learning about these "distortions" led to the bombshell moment and the recognition that *thoughts are not facts*. Because I thought these things, I assumed they were real. While psychologists and therapists disagree about whether to call these ways of thinking "distortions," it is a common belief that they are learned behavior patterns. And because they are learned, they can also be unlearned.

But that takes time. It is an active process of bringing what's been unconscious and under the surface to conscious awareness and light. This is more than "good vibes;" it is rewiring our internal programming. And this means we have to look to the past once again.

I first heard about one's "inner child" when I started reparenting myself. I realized that the things that often triggered me in parenthood or teacherhood were things my young self got in trouble for. Consequently, reparenting oneself is one of the most challenging endeavors you may ever take on. You're doing something differently than the way you were taught. Ever heard the term "healing generational trauma?" This is it.

You're giving yourself what you didn't always get as a child.[25] Often, compassion, grace, and the certainty of love. The aim is to heal the parts of you that feel wounded while not passing on the same behaviors to those around you.

It feels pretty easy as an educator, right? I used to think so! After all, you're a trained professional who presumably enjoys being around and supporting youth. But you can't see that you're working with past hurts in real time while tending to your adult responsibilities. All the while, you are trying to change how you respond to stimuli and stressors. Now, add in working with children or being a parent to your own children, and you're practically in a no-holds game of *Dodgeball.* The hits keep coming. Eventually, you may learn to catch a ball, but at the beginning, you're getting slammed in the face with repressed memories. They're coming so fast! *Ouch! No time to think—Better throwback!*

You may not want to be responding the way you are, but your nervous system is under attack.

Before I started therapy, I didn't know why situations like the one from my classroom happened to me. I assumed it was me (Taylor's Version). That I was just immature or selfish or secretly a bad person, but now I can see it's because of my upbringing and unique makeup. I've also come to see I'm not alone in these thoughts, as Dr. Kristin Neff's definition of *shared humanity* describes. Yet, no matter where they came from exactly—and let me be clear, the point of this is not to shame my parents, or yours for that matter—we can focus on what we can do *now that we have awareness.*

Once we have awareness, we can see what's been at play.

Like most of us who grew up with the Internet and are now using it to reparent, relearn, and uncover what's really been going on in our bodies and brains, I recognize that I had a "both" childhood. It was both awe-filled and difficult. It provided tender, heartwarming moments that still fill me today, and I see that there's also been a lot I am only processing now as an adult.

Still, childhood was magical for me in so many ways. Books like *The Boxcar Children* series were my haven. Trees, alleyways, secret passages, and forts were the adventures I lived for. *Harriet the Spy,* the *Ghostwriters,* and teams on the *Legends of the Hidden Temple* inspired me to seek, reach, and dream. For a whole year, I became the gymnasts Dominique Mochiano and Kerri Strug, constantly reliving our 1996 Olympic victory. There wasn't a patch of grass I didn't covet.

I loved being outside, playing kickball with all the neighborhood kids, the freedom that riding bikes with friends gave us, and the fact that I lived up the street from Erie's finest ice cream store, Whippy Dip.

Like any self-respecting 90s kid, my bedroom wall was plastered with no less than 50 pictures of Devon Sawa, with one corner rightly dedicated to the Spice Girls. I had presents under my tree, and food was mostly on the table. My grandmother adored me, and she always made me feel so special.

And..

Tension was another member of my family growing up. And in a two-bedroom apartment, there was already little room to spare. Often in the cramped house and shared bed where I lived, I longed to be somewhere else. I wanted clean. I wanted organized. I wanted something better.

As I got a little older and learned that some people have money and some don't and that we edged closer to the don't side, my mom and I would make a game of scouring the Sunday paper for house listings. "If we won the lottery," we'd say, envisioning ourselves in our *Glenwood Hills* house with an indoor swimming pool, five bedrooms, and a two-car garage, we felt free and at ease. This game went on for many years. Laying in the top bunk bed that I shared with my sister, I didn't count on sheep to fall asleep. I played another game, "Three Wishes," where you'd wish for something and then something else. Wish three always being, "I wish for more wishes." My wishes weren't of candy and electronics, things any kid might want. Instead, my wishes took care of the needs of others: I wished for a bigger house. I wished to pay off my mom's debt.

I wished to set up a college fund. I wished to buy my parents new cars. And, when I could, I wished for happiness.

It's not that I put others' needs before my own, but others' needs were my own.

Throughout adolescence, there was always an invisible pull in my house. Now, at age 38, I understand it better than I did when I was ten. As a child, I felt like one person in the mix of all my siblings, another when it was just my younger brother and me at our father's house, and someone all my own when I was alone. I was constantly switching identities and roles depending on who I was with.

At my mom's, I was Christina who was stubborn and emotional.

At my dad's, I was Christina who was golden and gifted.

To my teachers, I was hard-working, smart, and quiet.

To myself, I was extraordinary, theatrical, and creative.

Shyness followed me throughout my childhood, playing a game of tag I never agreed to. I watched from the sidelines, too scared to move forward, as my first-grade teacher emerged from the building on the first day of school, a story I've since shared with my own daughter amid her worries of a fresh, new year. Always the tap dancer, I flapped and ball-changed on any surface I could find. Yet, despite this passion, on my first day of dance class, I shuffled my way to the teacher's chair for the entirety of the class period to get away from the crowd. Leaving the safety of myself was too much to bear.

I didn't want to be shy, but I didn't know how to escape it. Adults didn't seem to know either because they treated me with reservation. They didn't expect me to be outgoing and loud. They put words on my identity before I could understand who I was. To them, I was Christina, hard-working, successful at school, and good at playing the clarinet. But also quiet, shy, and unreasonably moody. And because I saw nothing to the contrary in public, that's how I saw myself, too. In turn, it felt like no one really knew me. And maybe I didn't either. I was constantly fighting with myself.

My early experiences of not belonging or feeling confused about where I belonged followed me from home to school and back again. Just before I left elementary school, I was beginning to become self-aware of my social anxieties.

In sixth grade, I noticed how hard it was to make eye contact with my teacher and made a mental note to myself to work on that (it turns out, for the rest of my life). Later that year, at our June graduation, I stood cross-armed and stone-cold, rivaling Wednesday Addams for who could go the longest without smiling. In fact, after the ceremony, another teacher decided to weigh in on "my attitude" and told me how I *should be* presenting myself. My mom, the hero, overheard the admonishment and swooped in to deliver her own choice words. A display that rivaled an angry mama bear crossed with a sailor.

Still, it didn't matter where I went; it didn't feel like enough for those around me. Even if they weren't directly telling me I didn't belong, the constant questions of "Are you OK?" And "What's wrong?" and "Is that all you're going to eat on your sandwich!?" made me feel like I was doing my own life wrong. In late middle school, I experienced my first form of validation in the pre-teen mecca, *Spencers*, a store for oddities and subversive humor. I found a keychain that stated, "MAYBE I DON'T *FEEL LIKE* SMILING." My whole life flashed before me, reading those six words. I was known.

I know that my parents and teachers did the best they could. *And,* it's OK to notice that, maybe, instead of more rules, we needed more tools.

I followed many rulebooks in my time, both in and out of the classroom. I did the things you were supposed to do. I got good grades. I didn't get in trouble. I graduated and graduated and then graduated again. I did it all in the timeline that's offered. I even got married and had kids.

But with each new transition my threads became loose, unwound, and unbound. I had to learn, all over again, how to tie my laces. In many cases, I couldn't tie myself up if I tried. Other times, the struggle was too great, and I no longer wanted to.

I didn't realize I was even supposed to have tools until I began therapy in 2014, after my first very difficult school year. Instead, I leaned hard on character traits such as "respectful," "responsible," "safe," and "trustworthy," but I never knew there was more to emotional health. I figured that because I did my homework, got good grades, and could manage to pay my bills while still having some fun, I was doing life "right." But it wasn't until I felt so wrong or looked back and saw my years of quietly struggling that I realized I had a gap in my learning.

Naturally, I packed this with me to the classroom.

When I began teaching, I knew "social-emotional learning" was important. It was, at least, *a thing.* But I didn't know much about that thing if I were frank with myself. In 2008, starting my career, it wasn't really talked about. It wasn't taught in my undergraduate courses either. I thought it was something you were just supposed to know—or perhaps would learn—if you taught those *primary* grades. You know those *little ones.* With a fourth-grade placement my first year, I thought I could cut out the soft stuff and go straight for the meat: how to be a responsible citizen (it probably helped that I taught Social Studies that year.) I definitely did not foresee being a Kindergarten teacher the following year or the nine that followed it.

Instead, what was discussed in pre-service teaching and echoed in the classroom was management, rules, order, structure, routines, procedures, and what to do in the first 100 days or six weeks.[26] Ultimately, I muddled my way through how to attune to my students' emotional needs.

Today, it's common to walk into a classroom and see signs about "equity," "honesty," "feelings," or "inclusivity," or to have a teacher versed in social-emotional lingo, but twenty years ago, our schools were different.

Heck, prior to 2020 and the pandemic, our schools were different! I asked teachers on social media to tell me the biggest difference they see in classrooms now versus pre-pandemic. One teacher of 25 years, Vicki, shared that "in her district, the shift to focusing on establishing relationships with students and meeting their needs now comes first and the academic demands are second." She went on to state, "This is a very positive change!"

Conversely, another teacher, Barry, stated that "many have no skills, [including] cutting [with scissors], social cues, and problem-solving." He ended it by saying they're "not resilient."

What are you seeing today? Do you feel schools need more academic and motor-skill support? Or are you in favor of meeting the whole child—the emotional side—first? How might both be addressed?

These are the questions we can ask ourselves to point us in the right direction. Fortunately, they do not demand a yes or no answer. And while some are prone to either-or thinking, with a little nudging, they can land us in the "Land of And." How might we use our past to inform our future?

Being able to name my emotions or tell the parts of my life that have been difficult has allowed me to build the resilience I need to carry on. Additionally, seeing my children and students express their emotions so freely has allowed me to reflect on my own.

In their book, *The Whole Brain Child*, authors Daniel J. Siegel, M.D., and Tina Payne Bryson, Ph.D. have given parents and educators alike the helpful phrase, "Name It to Tame It," which means that when we state the feeling or give words to our experience, it lessens its intensity, and we can move forward. Siegal and Bryson write that "*coming to terms* with our painful and frightening experience makes them less painful and frightening."[27] Of course, their work is for children, but what works for kids also works for adults.

I saw that firsthand when I moved to California.

We gathered around the recess courtyard in one large circle. Students, teachers, and families grouped in their respective classes, and it was still one big community. This was how we began every morning: a school-wide morning circle led by song and affirmation. Over the years, it grew, and we moved to a larger part of the courtyard, but the implicit message was always the same: *We can do this, and we can do this together.*

The year the social-emotional curriculum "Toolbox" was introduced, it became incorporated into those morning meetings. The Toolbox Project is a program designed to build mindfulness, empathy, and resilience through the teaching of its 12 pillars, commonly called "Tools."[28]

In my classrooms and schools before this, behaviors absolutely were discussed because, again, classroom management was often seen as the hallmark of a successful teacher. However, the discussions were always about how disruptive a child was to others and less about what that teacher could do to support that child's well-being.

In Oakland, that conversation changed. We learned how to help kids regulate themselves. The teaching of these "tools" suddenly moved to the forefront of what I was doing.

Our conversations in staff meetings also included ways to support marginalized children, mainly how the more extensive societal systems that govern the world also play out in the classroom. We noticed that Black and Brown students got in trouble more. Rather than let that be the continued status quo, school leaders encouraged readings of books like Dr. Beverly Daniel Tatum's *Why Are All the Black Kids Sitting Together in the Cafeteria?*[29]

It was a 180 turn away from everything that I'd known.

My social-emotional vocabulary expanded, too, with new curricula and terms:

"Positive Discipline"

"Light of the Child"

"Zones of Regulation"

"Restorative Justice"

"Trauma Informed Care"

While a lot had changed around behavior management in my first six years teaching, including going from "Green-Yellow-Red" systems and "Names on Cards" to "Time-Ins" and "Mindful Breathing," I still felt perplexed by how much varied from coast to coast.

But I couldn't deny that it was changing me, too.

I began to see that what was happening outside of the classroom had a bearing on what was happening in it. I was able to break the barrier I put up that separated me from my students and their families. I began to see them as people, too.

That's what a true social-emotional curriculum will do. It equips us with tools *and* helps us see our humanity.

With Toolbox fully implemented into our everyday work, I couldn't believe there was ever a time when we didn't have a social-emotional curriculum. On open house nights, I'd often said to parents how I wish I'd been taught these tools as a child! I shared that these *were* tools I was using as an adult (in therapy, mind you).

On top of that, I expressed my awe that children as young as four were learning about their "Breathing Tool," their "Using their Words Tool," and their "Apology and Forgiveness Tool," to name a few.

To this day, I have a copy hanging in my living room.

Sometimes, I do have to take a step back to see how far I've come. Not only did I have to tell myself kinder words, I had to interrogate those thoughts and recognize they weren't true. *No, I wasn't lousy. No, they're not mad. No, I'm not a bad teacher.*

This mindfulness and attentiveness to my internal world was life-changing.

I used to roll my eyes at sayings like, "Live, Laugh, Love." They were hokey and trite, and ew, no thanks. I liked keeping my cool edge. Thankyouverymuch. But, by the spring of 2014, after a few months of therapy and intentional, purposeful watching of my thoughts, I had another breakthrough moment. I finally understood the word "blessed." Sitting in my living room, friends surrounding me for my birthday, I felt that warm sensation of gratitude. I was ever-present and open to the love before me. I felt as if I had unlocked a mystery of life. *Is this what people have been feeling? Is this what they meant?* Yes, please sign me up.

I was so grateful to be in a space where I felt hope, light, and presence. A few months prior were some of the darkest of my life. I didn't think this new feeling was possible. And here it was, mine for the taking.

But it didn't just appear on its own; it had to be cultivated.

I started an evening meditation practice, partly to calm my loud inner dialogue and partly to focus on my breathing. Like many things in my life, meditation had always felt like something great that other people do. But not me. "*Something so sophisticated couldn't be for me,*" I thought. I was completely wrong.

The first deep meditation I experienced was sensational. It was transcendent. I couldn't believe this access was available to me at any time. I was hooked on the stillness it brought to my internal world.

Interestingly, when I completed my Montessori training, I was shown a lesson about how to "Make Silence," where children are guided to take an egg timer off of the shelf and sit near their work rug with a card labeled "Silence Game" (game presumably added for motivation). It blew me away that it was possible to teach children these concepts. Something I came back to when I started this practice for myself and later when I wrote the affirmations that came to me in silence.

To help a beginner like myself, I played ambient "spa" music to help me build the endurance to sit for longer periods. The music also became a signal of rest. I found it took me to a place away from the daily grind. I'd visualize myself someplace calmer, somewhere more collected.

Some (more soulful folk) may say trying to get anything out of meditation negates the whole process, but I also knew what I needed. I knew I needed to find a way to quiet the deafening inner critic in my head so I could feel the stillness and softness of meditation's promise. Music or no music, I found what worked for me.

Now, of course, starting to meditate and sitting still long enough to feel like your body won't combust takes some work, some patience. But the rewards multiply.

One of my favorite Zen sayings goes, "If you don't think you have time to meditate for an hour, meditate for two."[30] That's to say, we have to make the time for silence if we are to receive its rewards. It's an active process. Of course, many of us do not have the ability to devote an hour to stillness, but we *can* find what works for us. And often, when we're most resistant is when we need it the most.

For me, this looked like sitting cross-legged and comfortably on my bed for one, two, five, and, eventually, ten minutes per session and, each time, building up the patience and tolerance to sit in the quiet and tension. That quiet space opened up something new in me. It allowed me to hear the voice of my spirit. The deep, knowing light inside of me. For me, this is where all of my strength comes from. The absence of ego. The lack of fear. A place of unyielding love. Simply me.

Soon after this practice took hold, I began to hear affirmations come to me in the quiet. It was like my body was telling me I was safe and that all would be ok. I was beginning to look forward to bedtime. Starting my night in a peaceful way allowed me to wake up with more clarity, too.

After a week of practicing meditation each night before sleep, a turning point occurred. Sitting at my dining room table, I looked up at the east-facing windows. A gentle light poured into the room. And I heard my inner voice say, *"I'm working towards being a more peaceful person who shows more gratitude and love."* Tears filled my eyes. Happy tears. Tears that came from a place that felt all-so-new and still as worn as home.

If you're like me, you may be reading this and thinking how great it all sounds for *me*. How could *you* possibly do this with all you have going on? Yet, I believe you possess this power, too. However, if you still find yourself wary, that's OK. This is neither a prescription nor a race. It took me nearly a decade of being in the classroom and examining my cognitive patterns to realize that *thoughts are not facts* and to find a process that works for me.

And, it's difficult to say any one thing works. Instead, it's been years of cumulative tools, strategies, lessons, and learnings to develop the wisdom to empower myself to keep going. It won't be any one thing for you either. But, there will be a first thing—something that helps you to see you don't need to be stuck anymore. Maybe it's therapy, or let's be real—an Instagram post—or maybe it's finally having enough life experience and defeat to realize those cliché sayings actually have some value.

My hope is that you will not have to wait any longer before you realize the power you have right now. The light in you. Your quiet, guiding, inner knowing.

What's waiting for you won't be nearly as scary as you think. Because when you take that first frightful step forward, you create the motivation to take the next. Soon, your forward motion builds the momentum you need to take the next one. And the next. And the next.

Emily P. Freeman, known by her book and podcast of the same name, *The Next Right Thing*, encourages listeners and readers to focus on what's needed right now to make soulful decisions.[31] The rest will come. Heck, in Frozen II, Anna and Elsa sing about it, too! "Take the next, right step" and go "into the unknown."[32] And how could we forget? Sometimes we just need to "let it go." (By the way, Toolbox calls this their "Garbage Can Tool.")

It takes more strength for us to cling to what isn't serving us than step boldly into the face of *New*. May we see that as hard as it is to let go of some things—traditions, habits, ways of being—holding on is actually what tires us the most.

After learning about mindfulness, I used that to believe you were *conscious* or *unconscious*; you were, or you weren't. I suppose there is truth to that on some level, but I see now that you are neither good nor bad if you're somewhere in the middle. When I turn and assess the path behind me, I see there's actually a third place: "Something That Looks Like Both."

In this place of both, we can see that it feels amazing when you're running on the highs of transcendence, but that's not a place where we can live all the time. You're not weak because you can't access that moment-by-moment presence, and you're not stronger because you can. You just *are*. As critically important as bringing our unconscious states to light is understanding that we can't, and won't, always be able to do this.

We cannot live in a perfect spiritual or emotional state. One does not exist. We can experience highs and generally have periods of equilibrium, but we are not guaranteed any sort of duration for their stay. The tension will find us because grief has our number. Living beings break down.

I've learned that the hard way.

These experiences of coming and going and my worry over being in the "wrong" state showed me how much I still had yet to learn.

Here's what I know now.

To move forward with grace, self-compassion, and patience, we must understand that the road will not always be smooth (impermanence). In fact, we need grace, compassion, and patience *because* the road is not always smooth. But how we carry ourselves during our highs and lows determines how we make it to the other side. Yet, it's not simply about making it. To paraphrase Dr. Bettina Love, "We want to make it and be well."

Presence doesn't eliminate tension, but it allows us to respond to it more mindfully. It gives us the power to decide how we want to react rather than letting our subconscious habits run the show.

That's what I need to leave you with: not the understanding that you're going to have great, fantastic days from here on out, but rather when they do come, you know it's because the forces inside of you are clear and present. And when they aren't, it's not because you suddenly suck—it's because you're dealing with a hard thing: Life.

And, as we're about to see, sometimes life is really, really, really hard. Thankfully, you don't have to go at it alone anymore.

Consider This:
- What are some practices you currently use that help you stay grounded and present? Which from this chapter would you consider adding to your repertoire?
- What does the social-emotional curriculum look like in your school? How have your practices changed over the years?

7

Maybe It's Not Failure, Maybe It's Burnout

Strength exists in places we can't always see.

The good days are good, and there's no taking those away. But, when you're in the ring of fire, and not the amazing Alicia Keys, *Girl on Fire*, kinda way, it makes the memory of the good days ache even more. You know what you're missing. You know what it felt like to feel good.

Add in some cognitive distortions, like "either/or thinking" or "black and white thinking," where you see the world in absolutes, and now everything just feels bad, bad, bad.[33] You may begin to question the ground you stand on. Maybe you can't even see the ground.

This work is hard because it's hard. It's absolutely joyful, as we've looked at it, but we are constantly bumping up against having to do *one more thing*. This never-ending list can quickly turn into a cavern with no end in sight. When we do not recognize what we are up against, we keep on trudging through. Only, in teaching, there isn't a finish line. You always have the potential to keep going. And so, I know you have. I know you are.

The years that dragged me through the mud weren't always due to a specific admin or one group of students, but how I viewed my responsibility to my challenges and what I see now are the pressures we collectively experience as teachers. High needs, mass shootings, limited resources... It didn't matter to me that those were obstacles. To me, they were just part of the game. In fact, I thought, if I really put my mind to it, maybe I could change it all.

When I held the expectation that I needed to help students despite the hardships that faced them or the systems up against us, I ignored factors that were out of my control. And it was difficult for me to see how I was impacted by holding the expectation that I should be able to provide for my students no matter what.

It's hard to change our old ways. Sometimes, we need a new mold. That's what my years in California did for me. It broke what I thought I knew. It cracked me to my core and let me rebuild on a new foundation. And with my "tools" in my pocket, I felt mentally equipped to handle the day.

But sometimes the tension will be too much. Sometimes, the tools will get rusty. They'll break. They'll be in the back of the closet with that shoe you couldn't find. And when we're here, we may find ourselves lost, too. Unsure which way to go. Wanting to be anywhere other than where we are at that moment.

It'll get dark. It'll feel like the light is out for a long time. And it may. But know this: in time, with help, it can come back on. Here's what that looked like for me.

During my attempt to homeschool my children during the COVID-19 pandemic while serving out a long-standing wish to use my Montessori certification with my children, I hit bump after bump after bump. Overall, Day One of "home school" went OK. Day Two had some wins in how I readjusted and pivoted activities. But by Day Three, I unraveled. I wanted structure; I wanted the routine, and I wanted to have it all planned out.

I wanted control! Parenting/teaching twin three-year-olds leaves little room for control. I was whipped. I couldn't keep up with the demands of my aggressive inner critic, who constantly told me I shouldn't do it *this way*. Or that I ought to be doing it *that way*. I just wanted to be right. And everything felt so wrong.

I wanted to prove so badly to myself that I could make this work, that I could teach my children. But it was becoming increasingly apparent that this was not a role I could do. After about two weeks, my days of being a stay-at-home-schooling parent fizzled away. I had held the bar too high. I was expecting perfection. I was hoping that it would feel as effortless as teaching. I didn't have the same capacity.

Before having children, I could leave my troubles at school. I could go home at the end of the day and reset. But this? This had no escape. No colleague to give the all-telling looks to. If my husband and I were coworkers, we were barely speaking. And trying to call home to talk to their parents was futile. *"Hi, hello, Christina? This is Christina. I'd like to talk to you about our daughter. Do you have a minute?"*

When everything felt so tough, I heard a sweet, internal voice whisper, *"Hi, me again! I notice you're being really hard on us again. I just wanted to remind you parenting is hard, and, also um, remember, we're in a PANDEMIC!* But I couldn't see those external pressures for what they were. To me, I thought I should overcome them. I thought I had enough "good teaching" in me to do a good job. But I wasn't looking for good. I was looking for great, for perfect.

I tripped over my feet. I stalled. I wandered off. I shut up and closed that part of myself off and slipped further into my personal hell.

Homeschooling felt like one giant mistake.

I sat in the corner of the downstairs bathroom, crumbling, with trails of tears marking my face. It was October 2020. Or was it September? March? The days all bled together.

I had just cleaned the toilet, and my three-year-old daughter was still refusing to use it because she said it smelled. I cracked. I couldn't take one more "NO" in my life. I already had to wrestle with withdrawing the kids from their preschool, my stay as an at-home-not-working-right-now teacher, and the follow-up but-if-only-I-could-get-a-moment-to-myself-I'd-be-able-to-plan-my-next-steps dilemma. The next steps that, just a few months prior, were all I could think about.

I had worked out of the home since I was 16, and aside from four months of maternity leave, I had taught continually for the past 11 years. I wasn't actively teaching at this time because my family moved from our beloved Oakland, California, to try something new in Vancouver, British Columbia. My husband had been working remotely for his company for a few years, and it finally made sense for us to move to Canada to be closer to his office.

And then, what none of us could have predicted: the pandemic hit. Just as I was finally feeling a semblance of normalcy from our move and all that came with that, the world stopped. Only at first, I felt relief. It was as if the entire population was suddenly on terms with where I had been for the past four months: isolated, alone, and with all my plans ripped apart. It wasn't the usual type of *Schadenfreude*, the German term that means to derive pleasure from another's misfortune; it was me finally seeing how much I had been in survival mode.

"How did I get here?" I asked myself again and again. Thoughts of regret and refrains of shoulda, coulda, wouldas echoed in my ears. It turned out the shoulda-coulda-woulda train never left the station.[34]

After I left the bathroom, I walked to the space in my living room that became like a holding pattern. "The ground will hold me," I thought over and over. I couldn't remember who to credit that to, but it was one of the more helpful things I came across on social media. A kind of post that makes those spaces seem so magical instead of the ever-present pit of gloom and envy.

I lay on the multicolored rug behind my small, blue couch. With my arm underneath my head, a single tear rolled from my right eye into my ear and then onto my hand. I lay there, and I breathed. It was the same week Ruth Bader Ginsburg died.

That week held many of the usual states, in their typical order: excitement, exhaustion, overwhelm, rage, sadness. Whenever I'd go outside, I'd feel a vice on my neck, a constriction, preventing me from enjoying where I was.

This had been happening for weeks. I was consumed by this block of what life could have been like if it weren't for all this sorrow. Even the windows were too vulnerable. The reality of me being stuck *here* while everyone else was *there* was unbearable. So, I came to the space behind the couch. I heard it before, and that Friday, I listened again: "The floor will hold you." There I laid, as often as needed.

Every day I logged on to social media in 2020, I was reminded that someone else got to live out their dreams, and mine were slowly, but fiercely, fading away. During this period, my husband would get so frustrated with me. He'd complain I was spending so much time, thought, and energy trying to change the world and that I wasn't even seeing what was happening in front of me. I wasn't taking care of my own family. For a persistent, wanna-do-right-in-the-world gal, I couldn't fathom letting go of this value to leave the world a better place. I was incredulous that he couldn't see what I was on to. *If only he understood me more, he'd see I was right in my heart.* Still, even I couldn't deny that all this energy I was putting into trying to meet my self-imposed goal left me more angry, bitter, and annoyed with my own children. Bemoaning parenthood and its endless needs became a regular thing. I absolutely hated it when I was interrupted. *No wonder everyone else can make their dreams of changing the world happen; they don't have children!*

My thoughts revolved around daily specials like: *Why can't I be a good parent? I'm so frustrated with myself. I mourn what I didn't get. If only... HELP! Someone, anyone, please just take my kids so I can breathe.*

I wrote this note to myself in August 2020 when my grief—though I didn't recognize it as grief yet—was at an all-time high:

> *I have intense bouts of motivation and energy. I can take on the world. I have intense bouts of depression, where if I could, I would lay in bed all day. But I can't, so instead it looks like crying and anger and sadness and grief. I have intense bouts of anxiety where I worry I am the world's largest fraud, I actually have no clue what I am doing, and everything I've ever done is wrong. I am away and I am close. A friend and a foe. A lover and a stranger. A shadow and a reflection.*

I have moments that toggle between remembering, honoring, and seeing my light. And moments when the darkness returns, because perhaps it never really went away. I have moments. Grand and small. Focused and hazy. Gloomy and hopeful. I am all of these moments and more. Never lingering on one too long.

Truthfully, I worried I might be over-exaggerating my feelings. Because of this, it felt so hard to reach out to others. Even those dearest to me. I filled my Notes app, Google Docs, and journals with hours of writing. Writing that might someday meet the eyes of a reader. Often, I'd hover over *Send*, but I'd stop myself. It all felt too dark. Maybe now wasn't the right time.

But eventually, I couldn't hold it in.

I remember the day so clearly. Kitchen. Blue and white striped shirt. Favorite denim jeans. Long hair. A crushing sense of despair and defeat. Somewhere between having an idea that would change the world and the actual world-changing, I lost myself.

I crumbled at the kitchen table. Tears silently streamed down my face while my children colored pumpkins at the table beside me. *I don't want to die, but it would be easier than living.* The thought startled me. Did I really just think that? The tears poured harder. *I can't do this anymore. I can't do this. My children don't deserve this version of me. I don't want to die, but I don't want to live.*

As a professional keep-everything-locked-up-and-deal-with-my-problems-on-my-own kind of person, my next step surprised me even more. It was the best possible thing I could have done. I texted my best friend. I knew that whatever I was going through, I had just reached a critical new level. And I was too afraid of what might happen if I kept this one quiet.

I reached out because I knew, from my struggles a decade prior, I did have people in my corner. When I struggled so much at home and work in 2013 and 2018, I was a locked cupboard. I didn't want anyone to see the pain I was in. Nay, I desperately *wanted* someone to see my despair, but I was too *afraid* to let them see it. *What would they think? What would I think?*

In the back and forth of deciding if I should tell someone what I was experiencing, I also recalled the bitter aftertaste of realizing that I could have asked for help back then, that I could have been supported when I needed it the most. And that my people would still love me.

But unfortunately, 2013-me and 2018-me didn't know that I could turn to others. I suffered silently. I hadn't understood the concept of impermanence, nor did I realize that long-term relationships ebb and flow like seasons and tides. Now, I know that highs and lows are the cycle and pattern of people together. But then, I went to work each day, trying to shut off my home life to focus on work. (I was *still* trying to shut off my home life so I could focus on work.)

Compartmentalization helped me for a long time, until it didn't. Until those lines blurred, and I felt more alone than I ever had. When work pressures ramped up, I felt like a failure on two fronts—a car careening who simply wanted to park.

Anytime I tried to talk about it, I choked on my words. I couldn't get them out. It would mean too much. It would mean this was my reality. I wanted to repair it, but I didn't even want to admit that it was broken. *Was it broken?*

Eventually, with knots in my stomach and being able to hold my breath no more, I reached out to a friend and eventually my mom, too. I was welcomed with warm arms. I couldn't believe I had kept this to myself for so long when all this time, they were by my side. Shortly after I confided in them, I began my first-ever therapy appointments.

And that's why when my tears blotted the ink below me that brisk October morning in 2020, as I sat at the table next to my children, elbow-deep in colored paper and Crayola products, and wondered how I could go on living, I remembered. By the grace slowly seeping into my system, I remembered that I had a lifeline.

Teacher, if you find yourself here, you do, too.

This is the teacher mental health crisis we've all been hearing about.
This is what it feels like when you go past your limits.
When you don't realize you should have limits.
When you've exhausted your exhaustion.

I don't want you to wait until it gets this hard.

So, let's breathe. Ask ourselves what's going on. Think about what we need. And hold on to our humanity.

You are more than this struggle. And I'm right here with you. It's OK if you need to take a moment.

Whether you are here now, have been here in the past, or live in the turbulence of being a human being, you're going to reach your limit at some point. Yet, rather than notice we need help and then do something differently, here's what happens: We keep trudging on.

We try to skate through the mud.

We shut ourselves off.

We cement this as our fate.

And before we even know what we're saying, we've called ourselves the F-word: a FAILURE. But maybe you're not a failure; maybe it's burnout. And as you're about to learn, burnout doesn't happen in a vacuum.

For me, it came in three strikes.

Strike One. At the end of the 2018-2019 school year, while I was waiting to board the trip of a lifetime—moving to Canada, getting to be home with my children, *and* carving out a new path that would transform my work with students and adults—the first strike came. My mother was diagnosed with cancer.

This altered our itinerary of how and when we'd arrive in Canada and brought on the start of many complicated feelings. I recognized that I felt guilty for being angry that this happened—a scratch on my perfect plan. Then, I was confused by my overwhelming desire to be closer to her (The "Land of And" hadn't been traversed yet). My husband and I decided to send me and the girls to North Carolina to visit while he stayed in California to finish the moving process. What we thought would be two weeks turned closer to a month.

Strike Two. Finally, together again as a family of four, we returned to the West Coast and began life in Canada. Looking back, my daughter getting car sick the moment the Border Control Agent inspected our car might have been another warning light. Instead, we were just thankful to have finally made it.

But I realize now how much I was waiting to "make it." I expected this transition to go smoothly. What's a couple hundred boxes to sort through? Unpacking our belongings also meant unpacking everything, which led us to this point. When our two-year-old screamed all night because of her scary new room, we had our first "*What did we do?*" moment.

That question rang through my head for the next four months. I became a mother who had difficulty transitioning to stay-at-home work. The overwhelming feeling of being unable to be the parent I wished to be conflicted with the professional goals I had for myself. In truth, I went from all of my buckets being full—rest, care, time to self, meaningful work, exercise, and a social calendar—to empty.

I couldn't pour, and any cup I did have was definitely not going to be poured back into me.

Strike Three. When it felt like I was finally making progress and speaking new words to myself, as in my Self-Compassion and Grace Journal and when I finally started meeting the people I'd been so excited to connect with, the third strike came in loud and fast. It changed our entire world.

Enter the pandemic. Enter the loss of life as we knew it—a life we were still trying to piece back together. This was the hardest of them all. No more foul balls; this was taking us out.

And then, when I thought we'd had enough and couldn't take any more losses, I reached another breaking point when we decided to withdraw our children from their upcoming preschool—the Preschool that only months prior we were so excited to have found! We couldn't wait for the community it would provide us. And I was so excited my children would have a chance at a Montessori education, a huge privilege and a decision I weighed very heavily. I felt gutted.

These discussions with my husband also made us aware of how we'd been operating on different playing fields. He saw my difficulties parenting our children at home as a sign that I didn't want to be there. Meanwhile, I felt pressure to find an income-earning job, believing my stay-at-home parenting gig was only interim until we settled.

But, so much of my frustration with parenting came because I had zero time and no bandwidth to put into any writing pursuits, let alone job hunting. This revelation was a punch to the gut. I felt even more alone. And even more mournful knowing that had we had this conversation earlier, it may have alleviated the pain and stress I felt. Yet, I couldn't change a thing, and that regret clawed at me.

As a former drinker, I find a lot of comfort and truth in the word "relapse." While I haven't experienced relapses in the way we think when someone stops drinking, nor was I ever in active addiction, my path to sobriety has given me new eyes to see the world. I truly appreciate and understand the potency of trying so hard to do something and then failing. Of feeling like you're failing. *Of relapsing.* Of doing the thing you said you weren't going to do. I've often written in my journal and blogs, "We can relapse in a million ways."

We are all human beings walking around with something heavy. Something we wish weren't so. And when we strive so hard for effective teaching, nurturing parenthood, writing a book, and remaining faithful, we feel the drop when we come up short in those areas we care so much about.

The Fall of 2019 and Summer of 2020 showed me that.

Every morning was grim. Before my coffee was even made, I'd panic about all that I wasn't doing. There was always more to do. Every morning, I'd resolve to figure out my life. Luckily, some days—even through tears—journaling and intentional breathing would be enough to get me through lunchtime. But by evening, I'd unravel again.

Looking outside sometimes felt like too much. Other people were living their lives, and I was so jealous that I didn't have the same comfort to be out and about during the pandemic. And I was incredulous that they were being so careless. *Didn't they know what was at stake?!*

As a teacher, even though I was out of the classroom, I felt sucked right back in any time I was on Twitter or Instagram. Everywhere I looked, I saw outrage, confusion, pain, and uncertainty. I felt so much sympathy for my teacher friends while feeling thankful I wasn't in that situation. There was no way I was going to try to return now.

As time passed, the gratitude for being a stay-at-home parent turned to guilt. The pandemic became another barrier that separated the old teacher me from the new maybe-a-writer-maybe-an-artist-also-just-a-mom me.

When you're in this place, someone telling you to 'self-care' or pay for a babysitter is reasonable, but it is also so out-of-reach. Because you know it's so much more than that. You can't breathe. You need a life preserver. You need more than words. You need help. You need community. But it's so hard to start anywhere because you're so hurt. So broken. So hopeless.

And I get it; sometimes it's just hard. Sometimes it's so damn hard. You're so mad that this *THING* is in your way. *Oh, I get that resistance.* I understand that feeling of not wanting this *thing* in your life. You're so angered that it's here. It was away, and now it's back. And you can't think. You can't reason. You can't breathe. You just want. it. to. go. away. RIGHT NOW. It's not fair. You worked so hard before. You don't deserve this!

What is this "thing" I'm talking about?

The long answer is: It can be a myriad of issues—a culmination of hailstorms and unanswered Hail Marys. The short answer is: It's *struggle.* You are struggling, and you can't find a way out. You're struggling, and you can't see why.

Raise your hand if you're here or if you've ever been here. Uh huh, keep 'em coming.

The kids won't listen.

You're overworked.

You're staying too late at work.

Your work never feels done.

Your mistakes are eating you alive.

You're tired all of the time.

You don't even have extra time.

You wish this were all a dream that somebody could just shake you out of. This nightmare on repeat. You scream at the grim reaper to go away, but instead, it keeps coming back.

The hard gets harder.

You don't have the energy to give at school. And you don't have the energy to give at home. You're in the fishbowl looking out, separated, deeply underwater. You desperately want somebody to put you in another tank. *Can they even do that? Is it possible to change?* No; in this nightmare, grim reapers like to swim, too.

You're one more disaster away from completely losing it....

Can I share something with you?

Babe, you're burned out.

Maybe you already knew that, but unlike what you may think, there is a way forward. When I struggled with my hardest hards and lowest lows, I didn't even recognize that I was burned out. I just thought this was life coming in too fast. I thought I wasn't up for the task. Failure was tattooed all over my body.

That changed when I properly learned about burnout.

Amber Harper is a certified Teacher Burnout Coach and educator. Through her own business, Burned-In Teacher, she has helped hundreds of teachers see, label, identify, and work through their burnout. I first came across Amber through Instagram. After talking and sharing the usual teacher chats—*What grade do you teach? How long have you been teaching? Are you currently teaching?*—she asked me why I didn't think I was burned out. I gave a lengthy response about my changing philosophy, my mom's health scare, the move that stretched us to capacity, and the struggle of the last three years.

But something was already changing. All because of a post she made. It outlined that there isn't just one type of burnout like I had imagined, but there are three. THREE! Even though my response to her still stated that I didn't think it was burnout, I started to get the sneaking suspicion it was—that it was one of the three: Burned and Unbalanced, Burned and Over-It, or Burned and Bored.[35]

I took the quiz on her website to determine my type of burnout. At that point, I didn't care much about which one I had because I was shocked that there were different ways to experience burnout. I was as curious to take the quiz as I was to take any personality test. *Would this help me understand myself better?*

And it did.

I was beginning to see that my burnout wasn't a personal failure.[36] A weight was lifted. I instantly wanted to hug my 2019, 2020, 2021 self—the me who struggled so greatly. I wanted to shake her and tell her that she wasn't a failure. She was enough. She was always enough. She was *experiencing* something rather than *being* something; The same way postpartum, new mama Christina was. The same way isolated and lonely 2013-Christina was.

I was not this thing. This thing was just something in me. And if it's in me, it can also come out.

You might think, "Wouldn't I know if I were experiencing burnout?" But the truth is, you might not. Because when you've been living with the water over your head, drowning becomes your way of life. It becomes *normal.* But, I'm here to say, this doesn't have to be your normal. There is another way.

I can say these things because I'm not drowning. And if it's hard to hear them, maybe you are. And it's not a bad thing; it's just what it is. Accepting that can be the first step.

Moreover, believe me when I say I understand. It's hard to be somewhere you don't want to be. I know how tough it is when someone says, "Just get out of the pool. Just get out of the deep end." What they don't see is this invisible force that has wrapped itself around your ankles, around your abdomen. And maybe you come up for air… and then get a cramp, and you're pulled back in.

So, believe me when I say I understand what that's like when you see, on the deck, a row of lifejackets. One says *childcare.* One says *self-care.* One says *exercise, food, talk to somebody, therapy….* And you just can't grab them.

I'm not negating that those things absolutely are what you need, but I understand how difficult it is to just get out of the pool and put on one of those life jackets. When you are drowning, you are holding on to thin air, just trying to survive.

You will understand if you're here now or have been here in the past. If you find yourself here in the future, please take these words as a care package to help you recognize the signs of burnout. Burnout doesn't happen in a day. It's through repeated, ongoing stressors that impact your body's nervous system. And that can be tough to see when it feels like this "failure" is all on you.

Although I lived in Canada during the COVID-19 outbreak, my entire life was in America. Because of social media and my ties to family and friends in the States, I felt constant anxiety, panic, and frustration about how the Pandemic was treated, or lack thereof. Being across the border was technically in a new land, but my homeland was on fire, and I couldn't find a way to break free. From school closures to anti-Asian hate and then the resurgence of a Civil Rights Movement, I couldn't breathe. I woke every day with a pit of misery. With tension lodged in my body, it blocked any chance of hope and light.

My disappointment quickly turned to bitterness. And then shame for even having the audacity to turn this around on me again! But one day, in the middle of all the mess, something finally shifted. And I couldn't have been more shocked.

While I was still months away from learning that I was experiencing burnout, I did learn something equally as powerful. It shifted my entire perspective on my struggle.

After months of hanging on by a thread, I came across an article about Spiritual Bypassing on Psychology Today's website.[37] It's when we tell ourselves we should "just be positive" during great difficulty and grief. It includes the fact that we often admonish ourselves for what makes us so very human:

making mistakes. When we spiritually bypass ourselves, we don't usually validate the harm or grief we're experiencing.

And that's exactly what I was doing. Learning this set me free. Truthfully, at first, I felt embarrassed: *Was I really doing this to myself?* But when the voices of judgment died down, I could see what I was left with: I was sitting in a big hole, but for the first time, there was hope of getting out.

Perhaps you're thinking, "*Can we just burnout and move on already?*"

I'm afraid not. That would only keep us in the cycle. Jennifer Moss, author of *The Burnout Epidemic: The Rise of Chronic Stress and How We Can Fix It*, argues that "we can better address burnout if we recognize the signs of burnout, understand its causes, and take steps to combat it at its roots."[38]

I see now that when I was experiencing burnout, on top of what was happening outside of me, I threw away my map and couldn't figure out why I was lost. I didn't connect those dots. And I didn't know a way out. The whiplash was exhausting. The yo-yoing was dizzying. It made it really hard to see the ground I stood on.

Today, I walk a new path. Two, in fact! And so can you. Pausing, asking what you need, thinking about what to do next, and reminding yourself you're not alone are the first steps you can take to stabilize yourself.

What's been most amazing and surprising to me on this "teacher recovery" journey has been realizing there are others who have walked this path. Others who are doing this same work. I'm not the first, and I won't be the last. Because when you get better, when you recover, you want the same for others. You want them to know their light, too. Many candles make the world brighter.

So when you're feeling alone… When you're feeling like you're the only one struggling—know that you are not. Not by a long shot. So many others are waiting with open arms.

This takes me back to one of my earliest and prominent school memories.

When I was in Kindergarten, my YWCA classmates and I graduated to the song "Lean on Me."[39] Bill Withers, the songwriter and musician, probably didn't know his words would extend this far. I certainly didn't think they'd follow me to this moment, but maybe he and my Early Childhood Educators knew something we didn't—saw something we couldn't. Perhaps they saw us for who we were and what we'd be up against. And now, I want to give that gift to you, too. So, friend, lean on me, especially when you're not strong, and I'll help you carry on.

And carry on, you can. But this time, it doesn't have to be alone.

So, notwithstanding the external pressures and things out of our control, how do we honor ourselves when we feel like *we're* the very thing in our way? How do we acknowledge we're in burnout?

We recognize we're hurting. We realize we need help. We understand this isn't our fault. We're not bad people (bad teachers, bad mothers, bad parents/sons/fathers/daughters) for having a rough go at life. While there are things we can do and must do to get out of the hole, for now, we can see that so much more put us in. Yet, with hope and with a plan, we can move forward.

As only those who have broken know, when you're falling apart and breaking, you get to pick the pieces back up as you want them. You get to put the pieces back together as you want them. This means you get to reprioritize what's important to you. You may eventually see that what worked for you in the past doesn't suit you anymore.

I came to see my humanity in a safe container to express my emotions. Consistent, loving, patient (sometimes grueling and disappointing) therapy taught me that. You taught me that. We are all influencers. We don't always know the ripples we create; we aren't always aware of who we reach. Maybe your words led to an act of kindness, which led to a post, which led to me reading it at just the right time. And here I am now, writing back to you. What we do matters. What you're doing right now matters. Even if you feel stuck, you are still making progress. You're still getting closer to the life you envision for yourself. In the words of my mom, "There's light at the end of this tunnel; it's just not as quick as we'd like."

But let me tell you something I didn't know: you cannot force change. You cannot force yourself to change if you are not ready. And believe, I am the Queen of Not Being Ready. For as badly as I wanted a way out of my grief and the existential dread I felt each day, my bitterness impacted my ability to see a way forward. I wanted nothing to do with this. All I knew was that I wanted it gone. Trying felt impossible. Trying felt like another way to fail. And I'd had my fill of failures.

But here's something else I have learned: you will change when you're ready. Yes, it might take longer than you want, longer than you'd ever imagine, but it will only happen when you've reached that place where all you can go is up. This may not look like a typical rock bottom. You don't need to lose your house, job, or family for you to realize that you need to make a change. But when you're willing to set down the weight you've been carrying, the bags of grief you've been hauling, you will begin to see the slightest shimmer of light.

This I know to be true.

You can't force yourself to change. You can't will yourself to *do better*. You have to be ready. One day, in the middle of all of your pain and torture, you will realize you can't keep going in that direction. Maybe you're not sure where you've even headed yet, but something inside of you will begin to churn. A new phase is beginning.

Welcome to The Season of You.

In The Season of You, all is possible. Will you get everything your heart desires? Probably not. But will you begin to believe you're worth the fight? Yes. Resoundingly yes. And this is where the magic begins.

Consider This:
- What comes up for you when you hear the word "burnout?"
- Who helps you feel your best? Who can you lean on in trying times?

PART 2

I Need a New Way

8

Understand What You Can and Can't Control

> *Breathe in what I can control.*
> *Breathe out what I can't.*

You've made it to Part 2. You've recognized two myths that have perpetuated our lives and allowed perfection to cloud our vision: "The Perfect Mother Myth" and "The Perfect Teacher Myth." You've begun to see how our nervous systems are constantly on GO and how our inner child, or early experiences, shape how we respond to situations. You've seen that sometimes the pressure will be too much, and it's OK to admit that. It's even better to ask for help. While we experience a lot of joy in our work, we also know we have a sneaky inner critic who likes to run the show.

You've learned how to identify this voice when it tells you you're not good enough. You may have even begun to choose new words for yourself, such as in a Self-Compassion and Grace Journal. Perhaps you're starting to let someone in on your struggle. All of this adds up. And here you are, still choosing to show up for yourself.

I want to acknowledge how far you've come. If we were to look at our "Keep Calm And" Path, outlined in Chapter 1, you've reached the "And You Can Do This" checkpoint. I wholeheartedly believe you can. We're not negating our bad days—the path won't take them away—but it will help you navigate them with support. We're not ignoring the curve balls life throws, but we're learning how to better play the outfield.

To do this, we need to bring awareness to the present moment, which allows us to assess where we've been and to use that information to help us make more conscious choices moving forward. Doing so enables us to see what *is* in our control and what is not. From there, we can decide what we want to pick up and, alternatively, set down.

As we've seen, 2020 came at us like a wrecking ball. We were forced to change our lives overnight while experiencing tragedy after tragedy. Parents, educators, and caregivers were tasked with thinking of their own well-being as well as that of their children and students.

If you didn't break down during 2020, 2021, 2022, or even this year, please share your secret! But if you, like me, were trying to remain alive and navigate your own humanity, you deserve a huge congratulations. For many, this period may have been the first time they faced *something out of their control.* How did it feel for you?

Perhaps I can ask it this way: Raise your hand if you've ever been personally victimized by Control? How often has she screamed in your ear to grab her? How often has she refused to let go?

I thought so.

Control is one *mean girl.* She likes to pretend she's your friend but secretly is holding you back from enjoying your life.

When you try to break free, she pairs up with the twins Worry and Doubt, and they form a blockade.

When you finally realize what's happening, you declare the friendship is over.

But that doesn't quite work either.

You find yourself blowing whichever way the wind blows. And you realize you do actually want—and need—something to hold on to.

We've all experienced Control in some fashion. I'm willing to bet you have come to know it intimately. Have there been periods where you clung to it? Have you ever been willing to discard it? How has your relationship with Control changed over time? What did that feel like you as you traversed those waters?

I always believed I had a healthy relationship with Control. It was pretty straightforward. *Be in control all the time.* There wasn't another way for me. Growing up, I equated control with responsibility. *I did my homework. I turned in my assignments. I didn't get in trouble.* When I began teaching, control manifested as classroom management. *Be in control at all times* still felt like the winning philosophy. Control was a sign of strength. If you lost it, you were weak.

But if we look at what we face, pry open the doors, and let the light in, we can see we've been under the *illusion* of control. In fact, author Elizabeth Gilbert of *Eat, Pray, Love* writes, "We never really had control, we just had anxiety."

We've been holding on to external forces, believing we are responsible for them, but in reality, they are outside of us.

I thought it would be helpful to review what we're up against to better identify if it's something we can influence.

Let's take a look at how we can use Control to our advantage, how we can develop a healthy boundary around this relationship, and how to move forward with discernment and ease.

Let's start with some examples of what's NOT in our control.

- Budget crises
- Student behavior
- A child's genetic makeup
- *Our* genetic makeup
- The absorbance level of those school-issued brown paper towels
- Rodents in the building
- Mass shootings
- A parent's disappointment
- A student's disappointment
- Our partner's disappointment
- Global Pandemics
- The timeline of grief

Yes, this list is varied and in no particular order. The point wasn't to capture everything but to highlight that there will always be much out of our control. Recognizing we are not responsible for everything can help us live with more freedom and ease as educators. What else would you add to that list?

It doesn't mean we stop fighting for what's right, but we recognize which game we're playing. It allows us to assess what's really going on and ask, *What are the conditions of the arena? Did the other team show up?*

Recognizing something is out of our control removes the pressure to be responsible for everything. As Dr. Sophie Brock says, it allows us to break away from internalizing external pressures. If we don't interrogate these invisible forces, we feel ashamed for what we can't do. When really, it's the system that's been pushing on us. Calling out a problem isn't the problem; ignoring it is. Moreover, if we can't see that our working conditions have always been the status quo, we can't change them.

According to the *National Center for Education Statistics,* in the 2020-2021 school year, 77% of all public school teachers in the United States were female. Inherently, this is not a problem, but what is is what happens when society does not treat women fairly or when policies inhibit our work rather than benefit it.

It is a national fact that women are underpaid compared to men. Even in 2024, at the time of this print, women receive 82% of each dollar men receive.[40] Minna Dubin, author of *Mom Rage: The Everyday Crisis of Modern Motherhood,* notes that this gap increases when women have children. But what she also found is enough to make our blood boil.

Women are discriminated against for prospective jobs even if they do not have any children at home. Dubin explains that just the mere idea, or possibility, that a woman could become pregnant causes HR to hesitate in hiring factors.[41]

And even if they are hired, they're paid less.

Sexism might seem like a current-day issue, but it has roots in the foundation of American education. We have to go back 200 years to the formation of universal schools and teacher preparation programs—programs that still impact education today.

Looking at how the systems that were designed to be "for us" actually went against us is one way we can see what's been out of our control. It's another way to bring Grace into our story.

In *The Teacher Wars: A History of America's Most Embattled Profession,* author Dana Goldstein[42] writes that as Normal Schools—the country's earliest institutions of teacher training—began to take off, they were done so at the expense of women. And we needn't look any further again than two of the country's first education reformers, Horace Mann and Catharine Beecher.

In the early 1800s, both Mann and Beecher believed that teaching should be in women's hands. Unlike those around them, they believed women possessed the ideal, feminine, "God-like" qualities that allowed them to be more nurturing and effective in working with children. Never mind that women could not enroll in colleges until the 1830s; it was believed that *if* they taught, it should be constrained to the "domestic arts"—sewing, knitting, cooking. It was a longstanding tradition and belief that higher-level work be done by men, for men.

While Beecher opposed this rhetoric and did not want to conform to the typical duties of a woman of her time—housework and husbandry—she still believed in the idea that a woman's place was the classroom. Beecher rejected the idea that women should be restrained to only meeting the needs of their children and husbands. Catharine Beecher saw how this limited a woman's access to the world.

Beecher believed that women could and should serve a purpose outside of the home. She saw their potential to do good for the masses. In this case, she saw it as a woman's patriotic duty to head out West and teach the uneducated. It's worth noting that when I talk about "women" here, that means white, middle-class women, a demographic that still upholds today.

Moreover, Catherine Beecher believed that women gave children their first moral stamp, an idea that historian Redding Sugg dubbed the "motherteacher." A term he believed encapsulated the parallels between teaching and mothering. In other words, they were the same job in different settings.

However, the implications of Beecher's and Mann's work went beyond philosophy. Their policies and pushes for a centralized teaching force of women still exist today. And here's the kicker: Mann and Beecher both advertised women as cost-saving hires. They argued, in addition to their beliefs about the moral superiority and prowess that women possessed over men, that it would be cheaper to fill schools with female teachers. And they weren't wrong.

Eleven years after Horace Mann became Secretary of Education in Massachusetts, he published findings that stated, "Replacing male teachers with female ones saved the state $11,000, which was 'double the expense' of the three State Normal Schools." $11,000 might not sound like a lot today, but at the time, that was enough to fund the operation of three teacher-prep institutions!

They advertised women as cost-saving measures because they knew they didn't have to pay them as much. Moreover, because women were positioned as better-suited teachers due to their "innate and virtuous" capabilities, hiring practices banked on the fact that women would be more willing to accept lower pay because, it could be said, this was their *duty* and *true calling*. Money? What money? That's not important if you're living out *your purpose*.

We got played.

Sadly, this is another trend that is upheld today. Once, during a pay negotiation between a former boss and myself, he told me he was surprised I was in it "for the money." In other words, how dare I ask for more? For transparency, I had the privilege and assurance of another offer, so when he was unwilling to budge, even $1, I left. It wasn't an easy decision, but paying women and teachers what they deserve shouldn't be so hard.

In his eye-catching and thought-provoking clothing company, Alfred's Laundry, Alfred "Shivy" Brooks creates living billboards for racial and economic justice. An Atlanta, Georgia educator and Atlanta Public Schools School Board member, Brooks, writes, "Teachers are underpaid because America does not value the work of women.[43] In addition to his t-shirt design, which reads "Teachers Deserve Better," the above quote on compensation is one of his most popular items. And do you know the number one reason teachers cited as a cause for leaving the profession? You guessed it, compensation.[44] The money isn't where it should be.

Today, it is easy to imagine that there would be a significant change in teachers' working conditions if the teaching force were 77% male. When Mann and Beecher pushed for the revolution of America's educational landscape, many male teachers quit because of the harsh conditions. Their calls for better pay, additional materials, and the strenuous workload were to no avail. The reality then and now is that we lack the needed structural support to do our job, and we're up against the expectation that we should be able to "do it all." The only difference is the men of the 1800s could leave education and become employed elsewhere. Moreover, their pay would increase, too. And that's precisely what they did.

So, how does this play out today? How does the "feminization of teaching" still affect us?[45]

Whether we tell ourselves this or not, the societal expectation is that we must be perfect. That, as if built into our

DNA, we need to be martyrs of this noble calling. We mustn't be concerned about our pay. In fact, we must carry the torch even if it burns our hands. As Mann believed, it's a woman's "true calling" after all.[46]

Well, we need a new number. And something I've dialed into is recognizing how much our capacity affects our work. When it feels like we ought to control everything in sight, no matter the hardship, it's incredibly helpful to understand how your capacity waxes and wanes.

In her book *Rage Against the Minivan: Learning to Parent Without Perfectionism*, author and mother Kristen Howerton helped me articulate a block I held for years since becoming a stay-at-home-teacher parent.[47] In her memoir, she explained how clumsy, unprofessional, and completely disheveled she felt in motherhood compared to her life in her former career. She wrote about how she thought she had lost her brain and intelligence. Only when she returned to the office could she see she was a completely different person from when she was home. She *was* still a person! With thoughts! And emotions! And interests! And a brain! Milk spills, sibling rivalries, and the carousel of needs didn't douse her fire while at work. She was able to see she was still, in fact, someone who had something to offer. A very intelligent, hard-working one at that. She was a worker at work and a mother at home. While they were the same person, she could now see that her capacities in each setting required different things from her. And she began to respond in corresponding ways. She could be one way at one place *AND* one way in another. Both were right. Both were true. Both made her completely human. Give and take.

It felt like a bombshell went off in my brain. When I could see that my capacity had changed and that it wasn't me personally failing, I was able to breathe. I was able to give myself enough space to break free of shame and make small changes. I was finally able to be OK with who I was.

I felt hope.

I felt like a piece of me was restored. Before this, I mourned the loss of my ability to complete thoughts and feel like I was actively progressing in my work. Then I guilted myself for this thought whenever I'd lament, *"But, Christina, be thankful. And remember, you chose this!"* I hadn't fully internalized the concept of "both/and." Truthfully, I'm still learning it.

But that book, her words, gave me something I'd longed for: acceptance in my struggle. The struggle of feeling good enough as a parent and good enough as a former/maybe former teacher. I held the bar so high and didn't understand why my arms felt too tired to do anything else. Why I couldn't do the things I used to... why I could barely hold my head up.

I see now that U.S. teachers who are also mothers face a double whammy in the challenges of modern motherhood and teaching: We need more, and we're not getting it on two fronts. If you're reading this as a spouse or partner or do not have children, this affects you, too. Remember, we're in the family business.

As a permanent resident of Canada but as someone who gave birth in America, it is mind-blowing to see how differently the two countries treat maternity leave and parental benefits. Currently, the Canadian government provides 15 weeks of partially paid maternity leave for the person who gives birth, with the ability to add on 40-69 weeks of parental leave shared between parents.[48] Given the United States' Family and Medical Leave Act (FMLA) only provides a staggering 12 weeks of unpaid, job-protected leave—which 44% of workers do not even qualify for—Canada's "extended" leave feels like an extraordinary privilege.[49] In reality, adequate postpartum care is a sign a country values maternal mental health and family well-being. It should not need to be a privilege. Out of 41 high-earning nations, the United States is the only country without a paid leave policy in effect.[50]

I share this because the effect of not providing mothers and families with adequate health care before, during, and beyond the postpartum period has detrimental repercussions.

My story is one of those.

For months after the birth of my daughters, I thought I was doing ok. From the outside, I was doing ok. Now, many years later, I can see how heavy of a fog I was in, especially once I returned to teaching. It wasn't fair to me or the students. I didn't even want to be there. And I knew the parents could see it. I knew my coworkers felt it. I felt like a washed-up version of my old self. Every day, I contended with the image of who I was before I had kids and who I was now. I was trying my best to make space for it all, but all I could hear was my inner voice telling me how much I was failing, how much I was losing, and how very off-track I was. And worse, I believed everyone else could see it, too. It only added to my despair.

And it didn't stop when my "postpartum" period ended. I include quotations around that word because it is a working belief by maternal healthcare professionals and advocates that the postpartum period is ongoing.[51] That a woman is forever changed by motherhood, both physically and emotionally. In other words, we are always developing; this is true no matter where you live.

After my maternity leave ended in November 2017, I regretted never mentioning extending my time. It felt like an impossible task, so my brain shut down the possibility immediately. I couldn't see a way for our family to cover our finances on only one salary, and with no extended relatives to rely on, everything felt risky. Instead, I returned to the classroom with resentment, exhaustion, and undiagnosed postpartum anxiety and depression before ever stepping foot back into my classroom.

That led me to wonder: How many of us are mothers? How many of our teachers have had to endure too-short maternity leaves or doubled stress when they returned to teaching?

To not pay respect to or acknowledge this profound lack of maternal and family health care in the United States would result in us not having a clear picture of the stress and overwhelm millions of us are up against in education. Both for ourselves and the families we serve.

It's easy to forget how hard it is when we're not in survival mode. And that's precisely why having a focus now can help us when the ride gets bumpy again. For me, Control and I bumped elbows again during my many transitions.

When my children started Kindergarten, I found myself at a crossroads. For the first time in three years, I had time to myself again. But I was also humbled by the disbelief they were in the grade I taught for so long. I had difficulty registering that my credentials and experiences did not match the output I was giving at home. For one, it gave me a new appreciation for all of my former parents! There is so much that you have to do between zero and five! I never realized the stress they were under! And yet, it was hard to give myself that same grace. I still held fast to the belief that because I knew the material, I should be able to do it with my own children. When I couldn't, I'd bemoan my circumstances or simply disassociate.

I'm sorry, what? You want me to try to teach my children their ABCs? Do you know my kids? I can barely get them to go to the bathroom. Give me a class of 20, and I'll gladly show them the way. But not here, not at home! This is hard.

This is hard.

Admitting "This is hard" was a revolution in itself.

One of my dear friends, Emma, and I often discuss the similarities and differences between our twin parenthood experiences and our teacherhood experiences. When her children were first born, we'd often have "walks and talks" over the phone to bridge our physical distance and get much-needed movement and alone time. She, still in California, and me, in Canada. Our talks paused as her babies grew to toddlers, and mine were deep into preschool shenanigans. But with my children now in kindergarten, we were able to resume our parent-teacher-twin talk.

As a fellow former kindergarten teacher, she was eager to hear about my girls' school experiences and how I was processing it all. As someone I've always admired, it felt hard to admit to her that I was struggling. And it wasn't with what was necessarily happening in the school; it was with what was—*or wasn't*—happening at home. She and I love literacy, and it felt difficult to say that even completing reading homework with my children was a struggle—a battle of wills. I was afraid of being judged by her, but I knew I was really afraid of my own judgment. When I finally shared this, we both exhaled from the release of perfectionism. The permission to be messy opened the door for her to disclose her struggles, too.

As high-strivers and people with a strong inner critic, it can feel excruciating to not feel like you are living up to your potential. I was bitter, angry, and confused about why things I could do a few years ago felt so hard now. *"Did I really change that much?"* I thought. And while it's true my self-imposed sabbatical from teaching did leave me with more questions than answers, I was also having a hard time adjusting to this new phase of parenthood. In rewind, I was having a hard time adjusting to *all the phases of parenthood*. To parenthood as a whole.

As a teacher, you are prepared for years. You are supervised, coached, guided, and supported in your journey from a college student to a preservice teacher. For me, my parent-training came from what I thought I knew about education and the conditioned beliefs from society.

I believed I should always like motherhood. I believed I should always feel tender love for my children. I should DEFINITELY NOT experience rage. I believed I had all the mindfulness tools and calm demeanor to handle difficulty.

There was so much I didn't know.

I didn't know you could grieve a pregnancy, a loss, a birth that wasn't your plan. I didn't know you could feel hurt by how your family responds to your parenting. I didn't know catastrophic events could intrude and loop through your mind. I didn't know that you could feel so much love and anger in the same moment. I didn't know I could feel so defeated.

And I didn't know that my capacity had run so low until I stalled. Until I broke at the table. Until I couldn't take one more negative comment to myself about my "bad parenting."

I had extremely low capacity when I was teaching and parenting full-time. I had extremely low capacity when I was pandemic living/striving/failing/falling and just trying to survive, let alone trying to care for and homeschool my children.

My capacity for what I thought I could do presently, based on what I had done in the past, shifted again when my kids went to elementary school. I had more time to rest, reset, and reapply myself, but for several months, I was cloaked in worries of yesteryears.

Are my kids excelling enough?

Am I excelling enough?

What will the teachers think of me?

Am I letting my family down?

Over the past few years, out of the classroom, I've let myself believe that teaching and the teaching world made me into a rigid and controlling force. I've wanted to bring the whole thing down and start anew. And I suppose in some ways I have, but not in the ways I imagined I would.

Interestingly, since I was out of the classroom, something finally clicked. I've realized how much stability it provided me. While so much grief has occurred during and since my time in the classroom, I've also realized how much power teaching gave me.

I don't regret leaving the classroom, but I more clearly understand what happened to me since I've been out. As a stay-at-home/work-from-home parent, I pushed away all the systems and procedures that kept me grounded as a classroom teacher. It's easy to see now how adrift I felt without them.

When my discontent with education caused me to flip my known philosophies on their heads, Control and I met again intimately. Control felt too constricting. Clinging to it as it pertained to student behavior, procedures, and interactions soon became outworn. I threw away anything that didn't fit me anymore.

I thought that was the answer until I woke up freezing one morning with nothing to wear. My back-and-forth relationship with Control was complicated. I didn't understand how one part of me needed it while the other wanted nothing to do with it. I didn't know how it could both serve me and hurt me, how it took me places and closed me off.

Once again, a model in *The Whole Brain Child* cleared up my confusion. Authors Siegel and Bryson use the metaphor of a "river of well-being" to help visualize our mental state.[52] It is such a simple and profound metaphor—and one that is easily adapted for a child's understanding! Within our mental health are the banks of chaos and control. Chaos is the uncertain wildcard, whereas the bank of rigidity is about mass control. They say that when you feel your best and are most connected to the world around you are typically coasting calmly in the middle. You don't get too close to chaos or rigidity. You can also think about this as *equilibrium*.

When I experienced the rough current of my children's preschool years, it made me think back to their words. When I ruminate, I constantly toss between these banks. I ricochet between rigidity and chaos, between control and free-for-all. It becomes difficult to find a healthy order. I can barely stay afloat in the midst of questioning my decisions.

That's usually when I realize I've lost control of my canoe. I'm a ship taking in water.

Siegel and Bryson further note that while a ping-pong off the banks is unhealthy, so is staying too close to one side for periods of time. Their words remind me that balance is key. These past few years of parenting have shown me how often I graced the side of control while thinking this was *Responsibility*. Conversely, when I threw Control to the wind, so went all my caution. In other words, when I notice myself entering into the "either/or" realm, chances are I'm not coasting down the middle.

Moreover, I've learned that the tight grip on control doesn't serve me well anymore because I realize it leaves me no room for errors. When I controlled every detail or perceived that I could, it was always my fault if something went wrong.

I could have done better.

I should have done better.

I would have done better if only…

Teaching held my life together and also broke it. It defined and boxed me and gave me the strength to see what else is possible. As I look to my future, I want to carry this lesson with me. I don't need to abandon that which supports me. It's OK to have control, and it's OK to lessen it from time to time. It doesn't have to be all-or-nothing. In the middle is where I ride.

In this seat, we're able to give ourselves grace and self-compassion. We more accurately know what we're up against. Grace says, "This is hard." And Self-Compassion says, "And it's OK that this is hard for me. I'm still worthy."

We can't predict tragedy. We can't predict defeat. We're allowed to have hard days, weeks, months, and years. They don't define our worth, but as I've learned, they can sculpt us into our future selves. Thankfully, another way to take the reins is to learn what you *do* have control over.

This can include:

- Our responses
- Our plans
- Our goals
- What we wear
- What we say
- What self-compassion we give
- When we leave school
- What we take home

- What we eat
- Whether or not we exercise
- How we treat others
- What we do with envy, with comparison
- Applying to a new school
- Voting
- Taking a break
- Taking a leave of absence
- Going to therapy
- Admitting there's a problem
- Asking for help
- Recalibrating our lives
- Reestablishing our priorities
- Remembering our values
- Learning new skills
- Moving forward with purpose

What else would you add?

There is so much around us that we cannot control. But thankfully, when we have space to remember it, we realize there is still much we can do.

I'm learning to control what I can when I can. I cannot pump budgets or ensure global pandemics will never happen again. I cannot predict when a health scare will strike or what new developments will cause us to shift our perspectives once again. But I know this: I've come a long way, and so have you. And I think we can go further when we remember that we are in this together. We are humans together.

After a tragedy, your capacity is going to be different.

After an illness, your capacity is going to be different.

After a life transition, your capacity is going to be different.

Your capacity will be different from what it was in the past. You are different now. You've learned things along the way and have probably let some things go, too. You may still be finding your way back. What you could do then doesn't define what you can do now. Darling, you are still gold, even on your darkest days. Your capacity will change again. *Impermanence.*

Another way we can hold on to our humanity is by honoring the profound grief we've experienced as educators. Whether it be through gun violence or the way loss curls at our ankles and grabs our hearts, we are still humans navigating a bumpy path called life. And because we are humans, we can grieve.

In the next chapter, we will explore what can cause grief in our profession. Please know that if the content feels too heavy or triggering, there is no obligation to continue. I'll see you again in Chapter 10, where we continue to honor our humanity.

While the next chapter will focus on the effects of gun violence as it intersects with schools, it is not the only grief mentioned. In fact, by honoring the many ways grief meets us, we can become more comfortable holding its hand. I wish to offer this path to you. When you're ready, let's go.

Consider This:

- What's something you previously thought was "in your control," but you realize now you are not responsible for?
- What's one thing from the list of things in our control that you can take charge of today?

9

Acknowledge There's Been So Much Grief

*I wouldn't let grief happen to me
so it came in like the charging bull it
is and said, "You will know me."*

I believe we've always been connected, no matter how your path wove towards mine. We've been pulling at the same thread in education: wanting it to be better than it is, wanting to feel better than we do, wanting it, and ourselves, to be enough.

And knowing that education and our personal lives haven't always done this, knowing that for many days or years, it's taken more than it's given us...that aches. Over time, that ache has turned to anger, and that anger has turned to grief.

Grief of not getting what we wanted.

Grief of losing what we had.

Grief of coming up short.

Of not being enough.

Of lacking.

Of failing.

That last one I know so well. Teacher, the fact I'm writing to you from the comfort of my home while you're in the classroom is the very reason that made me think I ought to have no business writing to you. It's what's made me feel most like a failure.

Once I left the classroom, I spent the next five years in a restless, unsatisfying state of determining who I was and what I was doing. Was I still a teacher? Was I actually a stay-at-home parent? Was I a writer?

This confusion led to longing, led to anger, acceptance, back to ache, and eventually, grief. And it's most important to say that grief is exactly what led me here. Reaching the bottom and touching the depths of my grief is also what led to my transformation. It gave me new eyes to see myself, new words to tell myself, and new ways of being in the world. This book wouldn't have and couldn't have been written without the struggle.

It's so cliché, but it's true.

C.S. Lewis wrote, "I sat with my anger long enough until she told me her real name was grief." I first read that quote on someone's Instagram post and knew I'd have to find a way to include it. It is what this story is, after all. It's an exposé on our anger, our rage, our *grief*. It was only when I finally began to see the grief in my story that I began to heal. It cleared the path. Maybe I can't change everything today, but I can make space for us to grieve.

Teaching and your identity as a teacher are among your greatest assets. And I know that because of that, this pride and weight we carry also has the potential to cause much grief. Whether through internal pressures such as impossible, personal standards, or external stressors, such as witnessing another national tragedy, a community loss, or having to pivot your entire teaching method due to a pandemic, what you are doing is difficult work.

Teacherhood and its wins and losses can also include the invisible labor of weighing the pros and cons of applying to another district, deciding if you should extend your maternity leave, or trying to wrap your head around caring for your students and your house at home. I understand the load you've been carrying. And I want to help you walk with more ease.

I need you to know that I see the work you are doing, and it is enough. *You* are enough. Our work provides blessings and burdens. Anger shows us what we care about. And if the things we care about are broken or lost, we can grieve them.

Not too long ago, I came across Grief-Support advocates Eleanor Haley, M.S., Litsa Williams, MA LCSW-C, and Mary Manera, MA of "What's Your Grief." They have an extensive website with grief resources, an Instagram page, and have also written a book by the same name.[53] For so much of my life, I thought that grief looked a certain way and that it could only come from certain events. Again, with the help of consistent, nurturing therapy, I saw that so much of my pain during 2020 (and in the decade prior) came from the sadness around not getting what I really wanted. In other words, grief.

I'm becoming more comfortable using the language of grief because it both honors and empowers my lived experiences.

Like many, I had a limited knowledge of what grief is. My understanding of grief came from how it was expressed in my family and in culturally accepted ways, which is also to say, sparsely and fairly non-existent. We often think of grief when we think of the passing of a loved one, but I've learned that grief can come whenever your expectations don't meet your reality or when you suffer any loss.

For me, being able to also identify my own "disenfranchised grief," a term coined by bereavement expert Kenneth Doka, provided much-needed validation. "Disenfranchised grief" is grief that is not openly acknowledged or that you might not feel entitled to.[54] This helped me to see that there were many events throughout my life, but in particular, this period, that took much away. More importantly, I had every right to mourn them.

Now, when I think about grief, I see it has a place next to joy. I see that "getting through" grief doesn't negate it, but it does mean I am growing more resilient. I also take heart knowing that when grief swells again, when I'm reminded or triggered by past hurts, it doesn't mean I'm doing anything wrong. This is simply the nature of grief. This is what it means to be human. To feel so deeply for the losses we've endured. And thanks to an image provided by *What's Your Grief*, I now believe that, contrary to what many think, our grief doesn't get smaller over time. We just expand and grow around it.

So, how might we make our lives bigger than the grief we've experienced?

Well, one thing we can do is S.C.R.E.A.M. because what we're about to get into requires all the self-compassion and grace we can muster. Next up, we're looking at the impossible yet terrifying reality that is America's obsession with guns and what happens when bullets replace books.

This is a hard topic. Be sure to check in with yourself as you're reading. If you need to set the material down for a little bit, go ahead. This is not a race. And if it's too much right now, that's OK, too. I'll meet you again in Chapter 10, "Remember You're Human, Too."

To avoid eye strain, I decided not to write this entire chapter in all caps, but believe me, I'm screaming. When our schools, students, and safety are at risk, it cuts to the core of our grief. Our fears are exposed. We're left raw. What's inside comes out, and what's outside comes in.

We can't talk about the stresses of modern teaching without mentioning what we've been up against. It's enough to cause our internal systems to ring the panic button. Sadly, you and I both know we've already been pressing that button for years.

"Be quiet! This is serious," I scolded the students, trying to sound firm but not too harsh. It is difficult to tell a group of five-year-olds that their life may be on the line. All they can think about is recess. And yet, we sat there with our backs to the shelves, eyes looking out at the row of windows across from us. The lights were off, and in between the breaks of silence, we'd hear a giggle, a *stop that*, and questions about when this would be over.

When will this be over? I wondered that myself. I didn't have an answer; from where I sat, all I could see was how nothing had changed in my eleven years teaching. I was a middle school student when Columbine happened, a high schooler during 9/11, and an adult while living in a gun-crazed country. My entire life has been preparing for one disaster after another. White knuckling the terrain of *Is it safe to be around this many people?* Finding the nearest exit anytime I'm in a crowd, and the panic of *Why is no one doing anything about this fire alarm?* Is something happening where we can't see?!

What *is* happening?

I was breastfeeding my daughter in her nursery, feeling the coziness of the brightly colored chevron rug under my feet, when I learned that a shooter disrupted a garlic festival in Gilroy, California.[55] "A Garlic Festival? Seriously?! We're not safe anywhere," I thought as my heart raced through the headlines. It wasn't the first time a shooting shot right to the soul, but I began to think the impossible. *If this happened in my school, would I— oh my god—* I could barely get the thought out. I looked down at my daughter and hugged her tighter. I didn't know if I could save my students. I wasn't sure in 2012, after the heinous Sandy Hook massacre, and I was even more uncertain as a new mom.

After Sandy Hook, school shootings felt even more vicious. They no longer felt far away and someplace else. I was states away in Pennsylvania teaching, but the weight and trauma of that incident reverberated across the nation. Shortly after that fateful day in December—a day which I'll always associate with the 6-year-old in my class celebrating her birthday—new measures were taken to up the building security.

Before, I could open my classroom door, but now we were told to keep it closed. A golf ball-sized hole was drilled into each door panel to insert deadbolts. I couldn't shake the image of Victoria Soto, the 27-year-old teacher who died while trying to hide her students in the closet. The only closet in my room wasn't even a closet at all; it was a bathroom. I imagined trying to hoist and shove kids into the cupboards that lined our north wall, but could I even reach that high? Could I deadlift a child above my head?

On top of that, I'd be faced with deciding who gets saved. There was only space for a few. I felt confident I could get the children into our modest-sized class bathroom, but then what? Wait to be shot?

It was evident we would need a different tactic. But instead of examining gun laws, we were given two green laminated squares. The slips of paper were to be put in the corner of the room that was furthest away from the door and most likely out of view. Everyone was to sit in the area between the papers. For my classroom, those were our northwest walls. Two shiny green squares of paper meant to protect us, to hide us from a predator with unchecked mental wellness, toxic masculinity, and a nation obsessed with gun access. About a month after those green squares were attached to the wall, we never discussed them again.

This is a burden we were never meant to carry. It is a paralyzing cruelty to expect children, teenagers, college students, and teachers to contend with each day because each day is another opportunity for someone to express their hate.

Now that my children are school-age, I have taken on the additional trauma of imagining something happening at their school while I am away. Just the other day, I was doing laundry on a Tuesday when the catastrophizing thought popped into my head. I saw my daughter's favorite teal sweater on the ground, the sweater her aunt bought her and all the cousins so they would match. I picked it up and was ready to throw it into the hamper. Out of nowhere, I imagined getting that dreaded phone call that there was an active shooter at her school. The fear and panic started to fill my body. *What if I wash it and that was the last thing I'd have of hers?* Just as I had held her close in the nursery five years prior, I snuggled into the soft sweater and breathed her in. I told myself I'd wash it once she was safely home.

This is the sullen reality that parents and teachers face on the daily. In May 2022, my children were invited to their upcoming school for a Kindergarten Meet and Greet. We were so excited about this new milestone in our family, which was still under the pandemic. As a teacher who spent ten years in kindergarten classrooms, I could barely believe my twins were now ready to enter that same grade. I was happy, nervous, and skeptical in all the ways I think teacher-parents are for their children to be in school. I was also anticipating who their teachers would be and what kind of experience the girls would have. But I knew I'd have to feign my excitement to help them transition. Uvalde happened the day before the event. I recall walking up the footpath to the school and wondering how it would be possible to have my heart walking around the world. The world that let ten years go by since the last elementary tragedy and idly stood by.

What I hate is that we can name these tragedies by first name but can barely remember all those who died, all of those impacted directly and indirectly. That list would be too long. Uvalde, Parkland, Virginia Tech, repeat.

One of the worst additions I'm making to this book is what I'm about to share here. Another school tragedy occurred since the start of this manuscript. This time nestled in a parochial elementary school in Nashville, Tennessee. There are talks about who the shooter was and whether prayer plays a part in the aftermath. But what if we didn't need an aftermath? What if there was a way to fix it now?

The day of the Gilroy shooting, still a brand new mom, I signed up to support *Everytown for Gun Safety* and *Moms Demand Action*.[56] I needed anything to feel like I was doing something. My anger, my rage, my panic attacks, and my PTSD of loud, alarming sounds weren't going noticed by those in power.

Teacher, I am so sorry that this is your reality too. It's *nuts*.

The day after this Nashville gun assault, my eye caught the label of a sandwich spread as I hustled to pack my children's lunches. The label for a product of "Wow Butter," a soy-based spread, read: SAFE FOR SCHOOL!

Safe for school, I thought. *I'm really glad we're so well-protected from nuts!* Angered, hurt, and frustrated, I continued on, *But are schools even safe for schools?*

How mundane and painful it is to cut apple slices over thoughts of whether your children will come home that afternoon. A poem formed in my mind:

But are schools safe for schools?
We've banned nuts
We've banned trench coats,
Shoes
And rainbow hues
But are schools safe for schools?

Extra checks and baggage claim
But ask me about my gun, and I exclaim,
How dare you?

Are schools safe for schools?

The package even comes with individual stickers you can place on your lunch containers, letting everyone know the food you brought is safe. Your sandwich is not going to harm anyone. Why can't we do that for people? Why can't we do that for guns? Why can't we have the same certainty and deliverance for weapons of mass destruction that we do for *nut-free schools?*

And the research exists. But the wrong people aren't looking at the right answers. As anyone who's lived on this planet for the past decade, you've surely grown accustomed to the chorus of "thoughts and prayers" after a tragedy. You know this isn't enough. And so does gun-rights activist, author, and school-shooting survivor Taylor S. Schumann. She wrote a whole book on it: *When Thoughts and Prayers Aren't Enough: A Shooting Survivor's Journey into the Realities of Gun Violence.*[57] Taylor recounts the horrific moments of that day in Virginia and the life-changing consequences that still haunt her.

Perhaps the most surprising fact from her research is that while school shootings take up the majority of the media's attention, they do not make up the majority of deaths from gun violence. Although school shootings are a focus of this chapter, it would be detrimental to not acknowledge the impact of *every day* violence from guns.

Because the truth is, the reverb goes beyond the shooting.

As Schumann examines, families and communities feel the effects of gun violence long after the incident. The wounds can carry for generations. Moreover, Taylor's extensive research shows exactly what can happen when proper gun laws are put in place. Seeing that data and watching lawmakers turn the other way is crushing.

As a nation, we are living with this reality every single day. In schools, stores, theaters, and fairs. At work and home. Perhaps the most chilling fact from Taylor S. Schumann's research is what is known as the Boyfriend Loophole, something that happens so frequently it gets a cute name, though this ain't pretty. The *Boyfriend Loophole* is named for the fact that women (and remember, that's the majority of us here) are five times more likely to die from gun violence at the hands of a romantic partner if they experience domestic violence at home.

Unfortunately, I saw the consequence of this firsthand.

During my third year of teaching, a kindergarten student I had the previous year, along with her siblings and mother, was brutally murdered at the hands of her father. Then, he turned the gun on himself. At the time, I felt I couldn't be as sad because she "wasn't my student anymore," but there's rarely a day that goes by that I don't think about her. Tears are coming to my eyes as I type this.

I'm not OK, and I don't think you are either.

After her death, I wondered if I could have done more. Were there signs we missed? *What about the day's Mom came in with sunglasses? Was that a black eye?* The little girl was always happy and cheerful. She didn't seem in danger. *Maybe we should leave it at that. Do we leave it at that?* What do we do?

These are the questions and scenarios that teachers face every day. Long gone are the days we just "get to teach." Our jobs and responsibilities to the children we serve, especially as Mandated Reporters, are greater than ever. And rightfully so, but that doesn't make it any less taxing or heartbreaking.

I've searched countless U.S. state websites and government pages and still have yet to find as clear and concise language around what to do for a child if you suspect a parent is experiencing domestic violence as I did from the province of British Columbia.

Yet, overwhelmingly, the research shows that children who witness episodic or perpetual assault against a parent show increases in behavior problems, anxiety, low self-esteem, academic troubles, and more.[58] The worst-case scenario is death. In fact, "one-third of children under the age of 13 who die of gun homicide are connected to intimate partner-violence or family violence."[59]

My student, who would be 19 today, was one of those children.

Just as Taylor Schumann remarked in her book, I, too, feel overwhelmed by such numbers. The gun stats are endless.

And sadly, the hole of the Boyfriend Loop is that women who don't live with, are not married to, or do not have a child with the perpetrator do not have the same protections. First off, for a gun holder or purchaser to even have restrictions placed on them, they need to be *convicted* of domestic abuse, which is a struggle in and of itself. If they are convicted, then, and only then, are they prohibited from owning a gun. However, if the abuser is a "dating partner" (i.e., the above living or parental requirements are not met), the same law does not apply. What we end up with is more and more violence against women and children.

If we don't take care of the mother, the whole family suffers.

Schumann writes, "[A] staggering one million women alive today reported being shot at or shot by an intimate partner." She also found that in 54% of mass shootings that occurred from 2009 to 2017, the perpetrator shot an intimate partner or family member. It's worth noting that in her work, Schumann provides more detail about what constitutes a mass shooting, as well as how the reported figures can often be misconstrued or misleading. In short, more is happening than we think.

This may feel like an "outside" issue, but remember, what's outside comes in. And we're seeing it more and more. It's the grief we need to name.

For another teacher in Pennsylvania, her account shows us what happens when the connection between domestic violence and the threat of mass shootings arrives at our school steps. She agreed to share her experience with me.

Darlene, an elementary teacher with over 25 years experience in the classroom, writes,

On May 10, 2013, a teacher's aide was leaving our school's campus to go on a break. When she returned walking back to the school on the front sidewalk, she was shot.

Darlene and the others in their school didn't know what was happening at the time of the incident. All they knew was that their worst fear had come true.

I was in the middle of dealing with an oppositional student when I heard my 3rd grade teammate, Jill, come running down the hallway yelling. I had to force myself to do what we had practiced so many times before. I was shaking so badly. At the same time, I yelled to my next door teammate, "Elena, lockdown! Elena lockdown!" I was purposely using her first name so she knew that I was serious and that this was real.

What started as a regular, albeit frustrating, moment in the classroom turned to panic in an instant. While my opening scenario was only a drill, for Darlene, her students, and the rest of the school community, their worst nightmare was just beginning. It wasn't a *What If* but a *Right Now.*

Once I had my door locked, there were some students who were still standing and talking to each other. I immediately started shoving them all together, yelling, "Shut up! Shut up! Shut up!" Once they saw me acting that way, they knew that this was no drill. I would have never shoved any of my students or put my hands on them in any way. And I certainly would have never yelled at them to "shut up."

The most vivid memory I have is when everyone in the class was silent, huddling in the corner; the only sound was the sniffling of a class full of nine-year olds. It still brings tears to my eyes ten years later.

I don't know how long we were like that, but the next sound I remember hearing was the sirens of the police, fire trucks, and ambulances. I was never so happy and thankful to hear those sirens.

After the incident was handled by police, Darlene's school spent the rest of the day on a "soft lockdown." This meant that students could remove themselves from the corner of the room but had to stay in their class and at their desks for the remainder of the day.

We were all so lucky and extremely thankful that the shooter never entered the building. The part that made it so scary was hearing, "He has a gun!" We had no idea what that meant. Who? Where? What exactly was happening? Working in an elementary school during the Sandy Hook shooting really impacted so many teachers. It was so fresh in our brains from everything we were seeing and hearing about it. To this day, when we practice a lockdown drill, I feel my heart start to race, and my eyes tear up. I hate the drills, but know that they are necessary. Hopefully, one day, our schools will be so safe that we won't have to worry about lockdown drills anymore.

It's worth noting that Darlene was a former colleague of mine. Elena and Jill were former colleagues of mine. I worked directly with the teacher's aide as well. This happened at my school while I was furloughed and working at Erie Montessori School. This happened at the same school my student attended when she was murdered at home. And the same school I returned to in the Fall of 2013.

While it may seem as if this one school is plagued or "at risk," the truth is these cases and violent acts are happening all around us. They are not contained to any one building, school, community, or setting.

From Erie to Oakland to Nashville to Newton, from Texas and Topeka, we live in a world ready and willing to pull the trigger. We are seeing gun violence, including domestic violence and childhood death by insufficient gun laws and improperly stored firearms, in all cities, in all states, all across America. This isn't contained to "urban" neighborhoods, gang activity (although many High School teachers do contend with this, as one shared with me), or communities of color. This happens no matter the place, no matter the race.

But no one's winning.

Gravely, we see this to be true: Gun violence affects communities. Schools are part of communities. Gun violence affects schools. Something's gotta give, but when? I know you and I are not OK. I know the victims and families of gun violence are not OK. And the kids aren't OK, either.

Nothing about this situation should be permanent.

And one of the hardest "ands" to say is that I don't know all the answers. I don't know how we get policymakers to look at this problem. But it's time we take back our power.

I don't know all the answers, but what if we start asking the difficult questions? The far-fetched questions? The things that are beyond our current status-quo? It's *insane* to do the same thing repeatedly and expect a different result.

We are a country gone mad.

We were never meant to live like this while active-shooter training companies, such as ALICE, earn close to $30 million each year.[60] That money could save lives and prevent further tragedy by properly supplying schools and districts with the necessary and highly needed mental health and wellness teams, buy materials, and fund school lunch programs so that no child goes without a meal. That money could do more than create more trauma.

I'm not telling you anything you don't know. I *know* you know this. But frankly, sometimes it needs to be repeated because this is what we're up against. This is an aspect of Teacherhood that does not get addressed enough. It's heinous and heartbreaking that there's a way forward, and elected officials aren't taking it. It's heartbreaking and cruel that they'd rather protect pockets than progeny; Grip power instead of people.

Jenai Auman, seminary student and author of the book *Othered*, a text on religious abuse, writes, "It's the power they really want—that power that guns represent."[61] Because isn't it always the control we are grasping for?

But as we've seen in the last chapter, it's not control we have; it's anxiety.[62]

It's true we cannot control whether a person will do something. But we can sure as hell put as many barriers as possible to preventing tragedy at this level. We cannot deny the cause and effect of guns and gun violence. Nor can we ignore partner violence and crimes against women. The research and the data about safer gun laws exist. Taylor Schumann's *When Thoughts And Prayers Aren't Enough* is one such text loaded with data-informed, proven measures that can and will contribute to safer communities.

The information is there. It's a matter of who's willing to look at it. And teacher, yes, we can be damn angry that we are living in a country where people choose to ignore it—especially those who swore to protect us.

Considering we act as mediators, consolers, and conflict-resolution facilitators between students all day long, it is unfair to have to solve this problem we didn't start. We are being attacked, and somehow, it's become our responsibility to bring all the adults to the table to talk about it. Only when we do use our voice to speak to Congress or our state representatives they're not ready to hear us. The conflict goes unresolved. When can we get the DOJ and gun lobbyists to conduct *restorative justice* with us?[63]

We are expected to grit our teeth and press on—and to our credit, we do. That's the stuff we're made of. But it's also incredibly unfair.

How are you doing? Do you need a breather? Do you need to set this down for a little bit? Remember, it's OK to go at your own pace. Honoring our grief and acknowledging the time it takes us to process difficult events is one way we bring more self-compassion, grace, and patience to our lives.

I recently heard a quote that said, "Your pain doesn't make you stronger, it's the safety of being able to express yourself that does."[64] That's what this work is. If nowhere else in your life can you express your fears and frustrations for what we are expected to hold, let it be here. I understand that you may not be able to share your views due to the threat of job loss, financial concerns, and personal safety. I get that. Remember, there's *Space for You* at the end of this book. *You are free to be here. You are here to be free.*

While not every act of gun violence garners media attention, I believe, without a doubt, each one has left trauma in its wake, from Taylor's story, to Darlene's, and even to my own. We've all been affected.

I struggle to write the following words because we know that our current cycle of gun violence refreshes faster than a webpage. Faster than the seasons change. Will there be another tragedy before changes are made?

But I think you need to hear this. I know I do.

While this is a problem we face, we should never have had to bear it from the start. It is heavy. It is heavy. It is heavy. It is a weight we cannot lift alone. It is not our sole responsibility to fix it, nor does this responsibility rest on you alone.

Furthermore, I've come to see, partly in writing this chapter, that I am not to blame for the death of my student and her family, nor any incidents of gun violence affecting schools.

All these years that I've carried the shame and worry that I could have done something more prevented me from really grieving that loss. Being present with you here today has helped me, too. Acknowledging I wasn't OK then and I'm not OK now helps.

Even as I sit in the grief that remains, I wonder how I should move forward. How can I detach myself from the weight of responsibility that says I have to do it all? How can I fight for the changes I wish to see while honoring my very own human capacity for suffering? How can I hold the necessary compassion and compliance around mandated reporting *and* recognize that the end result is out of my control?

When so much of what happens in the classroom is supposed to be in our control, how might we loosen the grip of that which isn't? How can I recognize that I am doing everything I can, and sometimes, it still doesn't feel like enough? Not when it comes to loss of life. Not when it comes to this grief we recognize as a genuine threat to our profession.

Gun violence at the local, state, and national levels has long-lasting, generational effects. Even for teachers who do not experience gun violence directly, safety concerns are still listed as a top reason for burnout.[65] If you've been suffocating and not understanding why, please hear this: You have been dealt a lot. And as a teacher, you've been expected to continue.

If you're only recognizing that grief now, take your time. It may feel contradictory to do so, but a body in panic cannot function. May these questions guide you, too.

Again, one of the hardest things to say right now is that I don't have all of the answers. More specifically, as my therapist would say, I don't have a magic wand. I cannot eradicate gun violence, Covid outbreaks, parental stress, and overworked and overburdened teachers. But I do know there are things we can do together. There are ways we can set boundaries around our time and expectations so that we can leave our work at work and end each school day knowing that we did our best. I truly believe this switch in perspective, coupled with empowering all teachers—seasoned and new—to value their personal time, will make greater waves than we can see at the moment.

I believe the way forward is to vote for local and national public officials committed to seeing systemic educational changes.

And I believe, now more than ever, teaching our children is one of our greatest honors *and* most difficult undertakings. We can only ever do as much as we can.

Lastly, acknowledging our collective trauma is one way we invite the grace, compassion, and patience we need to carry on. It equips us to care for our nervous systems by inviting regulation practices, such as deep breathing, adequate sleep, and time in nature, to calm our panic.[66] It allows us to soothe the parts of us that need healing.

So, I say this to you and to me as well: *Keep going, my love. You are making moves. Your ripples will wash the feet of generations to come. I believe this wholeheartedly.*

Consider This:

- Naming our grief allows us to heal. What in your Teacherhood experience has brought on the most grief? Contrary to what many believe, grief is rarely linear, nor does it ever fully go away. How might you find ways to grow around your grief? Are there ceremonies or traditions that help you connect with your grief?
- It may feel contradictory to give yourself time to grieve when so much is on the line, but a body in panic cannot function. How might you remember you're capable of small, courageous acts while still honoring your body's need to stabilize your nervous system?

10

Remember, You're Human Too

When I set down what was never mine to carry, I became free.

I believe we need to equip teachers, new and seasoned, parents or not, with the knowledge of what they're getting into and what to expect—what to really expect. When we do this, we're not telling them to "just deal with it;" we're setting them up for true success because there's more transparency.

And I get it. It might be scary. It might deter prospective teachers from even entering the field. But wouldn't you have liked to know?

Laying out the realities of modern teaching might not give us the same number of teachers entering the profession, but we wouldn't have the same number leaving. *Remember, we're not just in a teacher shortage. We're in a shortage of teacher care.* Wouldn't it have been instructive for someone to tell you there will be so many amazing days, but alongside those, there will also be the defeating ones? And that this is OK?! *Impermanence.*

Might that have helped you to lower the high expectations you have for yourself?

And when things become difficult, your first thought wouldn't be, *"I'm a failure."* Perhaps it could be, *"Wow, this is really hard. What should I do now?"* or, *"Whom might I ask for help?"* And then, with open arms, another teacher could be there to hold you. Or you for them. Or you, for yourself.

Normalizing the bad doesn't make us condone it, but it allows us to better meet it when it comes. So, let's look again at what's going on in classrooms today and how these daily high needs have impacted our sense of responsibility and, in turn, our sense of adequacy.

Teachers have struggled with behaviors since the beginning of formal education. Yet it never occurred to me, until it was taught during an in-service day in 2016, that so much of what we encounter in the classroom is trauma—something we are only beginning to understand.

As teachers, we are expected to welcome and hold whatever and whoever comes through our door. No matter their level, no matter their range, no matter what day, color T-shirt, bad mood, or system at our back, we are meant to educate them—and educate them well. That is our pride and duty, and for all intents and purposes, what constitutes our training.

However, with so much teacher preparation discussing the best classroom management techniques, it's easy to see how this communicated to the teacher that they're responsible for the behavior and actions of others. No matter the behavior.

While I spent much of my career believing it was paramount for me to manage my class, which, of course, *it is*, I am only now seeing how much I internalized the belief that I was a bad teacher if I couldn't.

When I encountered five-year-olds who swore, hit, and kicked and who displayed their frustrations by throwing around classroom materials, my first reaction wasn't, *"How do I help this child?"* it was, *"OMG, I am failing this child,"* followed by, *"I am a bad teacher."*

Moreover, in the last few years, I've seen how wrongly I associated certain behaviors as "bad." Even if I wasn't saying the child was bad, I was saying they were *acting bad.* They were making *a bad choice.* But is it a choice? When a child lacks the emotional regulation to access reason and logic, are they choosing to be disruptive?[67] Could it be something more? And if it's not a choice for them, then who is responsible?

Welcome to the world of "ACEs," aka what we teachers meet on the daily. The elephants in the room we are only beginning to truly see and understand.

I didn't learn about the term ACES, or Adverse Childhood Experiences, until 2016, ten years after I set foot in my first preservice field training. Adverse Childhood Experiences is a term created in 1995 by a team of researchers at the CDC and Kaiser Permanente-California, and includes "things like physical and emotional abuse, neglect, caregiver mental illness, and household violence." It was studied that the more ACES a child has, the more likely it is for them to suffer from illnesses such as heart disease, school-related learning difficulties, and substance abuse or addiction.[68]

My bookshelf is still lined with my beloved education resources from college, many of which I still reference, but a chapter in a textbook about ADHD, childhood neglect, or physical differences isn't the same as meeting the children experiencing those circumstances with empathy and working with them effectively. It takes ongoing professional development around trauma-informed care and practices, which was not taught in my teacher preparation courses. However, even if we receive that training, which varies widely between districts and states, it can often feel like too little, too late. Or it becomes an issue of not enough staff. Who is helping the students and teacher through the crisis? What's going on with the 25 other children? Because you're not just failing a product if you don't succeed, you're failing a person.

At least that's what I believed. So, when I couldn't meet the needs of the children in my classroom, I didn't blame the system and its lack of resources; I blamed myself.

Additionally, because I put so much pressure on myself to perform—and because classroom management and perceived control were hallmarks of a successful teacher—I felt guilt and shame for not being able to help these children during their emotional outbursts. If I became triggered, raised my voice, showed my own frustrations, or felt inner rage, the shame built even more. "Bad teacher" for sure.

The truth is, we are slammed with high emotional needs and few resources to meet students where they're at, ACEs or not, trauma or not. And sometimes, it just doesn't seem fair—to us or the students. We still operate in an education model that penalizes schools and districts for not meeting benchmark indicators, although the financial support needed to uplift our children is entirely vacant. We admonish "at risk" schools and learners but provide little help. Unfortunately, this doesn't result in a criticism of the system but of the teacher.*[69]

We are expected to fill continent-sized gaps between students without the proper resources. And the academic range between learners can be massive. One year, I had a kindergarten student reading *Harry Potter,* while another couldn't even write his name. This is not a judgment or a mark on either of those students or their families but acknowledgement that we are expected to fill the canyon between two mountains.

It's impossible to know it all your first year. Or even your tenth! It takes trial. It takes error. That's hard to admit when you're in the people business. When it feels like you ought to meet everyone's needs all of the time. And as a teacher, you are front row to the carousel of needs, never without a ticket to the *not-so*-merry-go-round of real-time scarcity and overwhelm.

Thankfully, the conversation around what is best for children continues to evolve. The conversations around mental health are shifting, too. We're recognizing that behaviors are a call for help, not the sign of a bad child (or a bad teacher).

But we recognize there's still an elephant in the room. It whispers you have to provide everything for your students: safety, shelter, love, support, guidance, meter, scholastics, mathematics, spelling, handwriting, social studies, science, emotional support, and you have to do that whether they're at A or Z. Whether they are above grade level or below. You are expected to do it all.

And for so long, I believed them. I believed we were expected to pick up the so-called "slack." I believed we were expected and expected and expected to fill, fill, fill. We had to do this because it's our job, which makes us a failure if we cannot perform miracles. The elephant isn't asking how to make our jobs easier; it's only expecting us to be more effective.

As a beginning teacher, I thought it my duty to ensure that I didn't *'leave any child behind.'* Knowing what I do now, I realize that even then, I wasn't able to keep up. I put so much pressure on myself to ensure that I wasn't failing the students that I ultimately ended up failing myself.

I set the bar too high, but no one told me to lower it.

For so long, I believed it was my job to be effective. In many ways, I still do. But I see it differently now. As a preservice field student, I recall one of my Cooperative Teachers, the teacher leading the classroom where I completed my practicum, cautioning me that "we teach students, not subjects." Truthfully, I felt annoyed at her comment. *She didn't know me!* Initially, it made me feel like I was missing a central piece of teaching, that I didn't have the true heart of a teacher.

When I was face to face with the needs of thirty children, some days felt more like triage: *Who needs the most help today?* Beyond teaching phonemic awareness and thinking about what lessons I needed to present, I was aware that I was doing so against the backdrop of poverty, special needs, disabilities, learning differences, students with ADHD, behavioral concerns, cultural and linguistic diversity, childhood neglect, and abuse. And the list goes on.

Nonetheless, I saw these as problems to overcome rather than people I needed to help. I figured I would teach the content first and the child second.

Seventeen years later, I can admit my former cooperative teacher was onto something. Not that I didn't have the heart of a teacher, but that my priorities were whacked.

And it's motherhood once again that gave me a new perspective.

Parenting twins has opened my eyes to what I had been holding as a teacher. I can't meet all my children's needs, especially at the same time. There will be disappointment on both sides—mine and theirs—whether I do something or not! I cannot meet their needs if I am unwilling to see who they are as people first.

Parenthood is vastly different from teaching. Being a teacher is different from being a parent, but parenthood has humbled me in all the ways teaching couldn't. Parenthood has shown me just how hard it is to work with children, especially when you have limited resources and things like global Pandemics. This is another aspect of Teacherhood akin to parenthood or motherhood: there will be things you will love about it and things you will hate.

I fiercely love my children and often need some space from them. When I think about it, I got into education for the kids, but I never realized what that would mean and how much it would take. It's something I can only see now. If you're a parent, you may recognize that same sentiment.

So much of my grief from 2019 on came from feeling like I had to hold it all. I was so upset that I couldn't do the very things I wanted to try to teach others. I wanted to teach them how to get out of the way of kids. I wanted to change the status quo for the better. I wanted to show them how to transform themselves so they could transform their teaching.

Moreover, what happened at home directly impacted my decision to return to the classroom. I was failing miserably in all the ways I wanted to change classrooms, but I could not see a way forward. *"I haven't learned enough yet,"* I told myself. I hadn't learned enough about this transformation I wanted so badly to happen. I was afraid that if I went back to the classroom prematurely, I would just fall back on old habits that worked, *NOT* those I was trying to evolve and co-create.

Secondly, and perhaps more importantly, I had zero capacity; I had nothing left to give.

I was caught between then and now. Between Teacher Christina and Parent Christina. Caught between how I wanted to change and by what continued to trip me up. I was in that liminal space we often hear about—that place where you're between two points. From a spiritual standpoint, it's a place of blessings—of acceptance. But I wasn't there yet. Grace and I hadn't become friends yet.

Slowly, though, Patience found a way to settle in.

The seasons passed, and before I knew it, 2020 was finally over. Spring of 2021 felt like the coolest sip of water. I still fielded questions about whether I would return to education, but I could say, "I don't know," with less backstory and care. I still kept a hand on my degree and served as president of my children's parent-participation preschool. Honestly, it was still a very trying year of juggling my desire to help the teachers while also managing logistical needs.

But I noticed the biggest change came in doing nothing at all—in taking things off of my plate and setting down expectations.

For months after our move, I mourned the loss of my book idea. Eventually, for the sake of my health and well-being, I had to put it to rest. But truthfully, I had to put *best* to rest. In pursuit of the best educational and parenting philosophy, I drowned. The idea I had to change education took me out of education. Because I realized it wasn't much of an idea as an ideal.

It took many months and much retrospection for me to see a sparkle of success in my homeschooling endeavors of the prior year. I became less concerned about my book idea. As Gotye sings, it was like "someone I used to know."[70] I wasn't quite her anymore, but not someone entirely new yet, either. I could finally utter that I was proud of trying something I had always wanted to do. In time and with more counseling, my therapist helped me to see that "Teacher Me" and "Parent Me" have similar qualities, but they are not necessarily the same.

They don't operate the same. They don't always want the same. Nor do their capacities run the same!

Maybe I'm still trying to justify my missteps, my balls dropped, maybe it's both, but I'm also trying to see, perhaps, this is the work that always had to come first. I couldn't write a book about the perfect education system when I hadn't dealt with what was getting in my way. I couldn't write a book about the perfect education system because there isn't one. There wasn't one in 2013, there wasn't one in 2018, and there still isn't one today.

For so long, I thought you couldn't be "an expert" if you got it wrong. That's why I so love and appreciate what Katherine Morgan Shafler discusses in her book, *The Perfectionist's Guide To Losing Control*: the idea that experts aren't people who never make mistakes but instead are people who are willing to learn and revise their approach (especially in their area of expertise) when new information has come in.[71]

New information has slowly trickled in.

We forget that schools are full of human beings. Our society has become so conditioned to see failure instead of fruit. *We* have been conditioned, especially as high performers, to see what still needs to be achieved rather than what's already been accomplished. And when things do go wrong, we blame the person and not the system.

While we cannot change our educational landscape without voting, we can decide to stop playing by their rules. We do this by showing up daily with the knowledge that we are Changemakers. We are a collective who can work together to bring change.

This is not superfluous or an empty platitude to tell you to stay or to ignore the importance of revenue streams or harsh conditions, but a reminder that every day, no matter what they say, we still get to choose what we see. And I see you. I see your hard work. I see the frustration of not having the resources or the capacity to reach every child the way you wish. I still see you doing your best. At the end of the day, that is all any of us are ever doing. Kids included.

But it took some time for me to realize that. It wasn't until I set down what I could no longer carry that I became free to fill with new things.

Free to choose what I wanted.

Free to be angry, upset, and righteous.

Free to hope.

Free to heal.

I dropped the facade I was doing OK, and through the process of therapy and medication and being honest about where I was, I did actually become OK.

Eventually, I had to make a choice. I had to accept that I was doing the best I could do. And that I was never going to be the parent I thought I'd be. Giving myself this grace and this permission to be human still reverberates today. I had to decide for myself what my parenting would look like. But more than that, I had to accept that what I could do as a teacher—with other people's children—was not, and is not, the same I can do with my own. This does not invalidate me. Instead, it finally paved the way to give myself the grace, compassion, and patience needed to carry on in the hard times.

So what am I doing instead? When doubt creeps in, I'm working on reframing my conditioned thoughts and asking, *"What if the doubt is there to teach us?" "What if we could learn to trust the doubt?"* Really, what if we could trust it? What might it tell us? Because *what if you did know?* What if you weren't worried about getting it wrong and you went with what felt right?

Yet, sometimes, in the midst of doubt, worry, and anxiety, we need a force more powerful than us to bring us back to reality. We need a way to overcome the hurdle in front of us (and the 100 others we see down the lane). We need something that's soft and gentle but with the strength and imagination of a new way.

And that leads us to five Radical Beliefs you can start using today. Combining the teachings, anecdotes, and stories in this book, along with the padding needed to continue, the following five statements have the power to change your potential. They chisel at what was and make way for something new.

They challenge held beliefs you've had to co-create a different future. Mostly, they can take you out of overwhelm and into ease.

Radical Belief #1
We are only ever doing the best we can.

To move forward in doubt, you must believe you're doing your best; this allows grace to shift our perspective on our mishaps and move us forward with more self-compassion.

Of course, I'm not the first person to ever learn this message. Chances are, you've heard similar words from Maya Angelou: "Do the best you can until you know better. Then, when you know better, do better." Her eloquence reminds you that you do not need to be perfect. It's OK to live and be human. Which brings us to…

Radical Belief #2

I'm not trying to screw up my life.

When we find ourselves on the brink of a decision, and we're not sure what to do, the anxiety rushing to our critical brain tells us: *How dare you make this decision when you don't know the best way to proceed?!*

This imposter syndrome, combined with decision paralysis, leaves us stuck. We're trapped in our worry and fear of failure. When we loosen ourselves from the unhelpful belief that somehow, by not having the answers to every single problem in the world, we're actively trying to sabotage ourselves, we free ourselves to be human. Even when you're unsure, you can trust that you're not actively trying to mess up your life. No one is.

Radical Belief #3

This is all that exists now.

Making a mistake when we're prone to avoiding mistakes may cause the Cascade of Failure to rain down. Suddenly, every mistake or bad memory loops in a musically-aligned montage. But it's not beautiful—it's a nightmare! It doesn't just feel like you made *one* mistake; it feels like you've been living a lifetime of mistakes. And they all matter! And they were all so important! This level of rumination is unlikely to go away on its own unless we intercept it with a more agile mind.

Radical Belief #3 brings all the mindfulness to the yard. It calls out everything that's not in the present moment. And, if we're strong enough, we even get to harness our Oprah power, telling each thought not steeped in the present moment: *And YOU get to leave! And YOU get to leave! And YOU get to leave.* We swat away anything that's not serving us right now—any past regret or future worry. We don't live there. You're not devaluing your mistakes; you're simply not letting them dictate how you move presently.

Radical Belief #4
It's OK to be different.

It's OK to be different because it's OK to be you. Somewhere along the way, you've forgotten how much wisdom, strength, and expertise you have.

You can choose your own path. It doesn't have to be for every decision. It doesn't even need to be permanent. But you owe it to yourself to listen to your own voice. When you confidently live in YOU, the world will become more open. You became a more open human.

Radical Belief #5
Joy is my birthright.

Joy deserves as much space as breath. It keeps us going. Without it, the world would be unsustainable. Like presence, joy is always waiting for us. It never goes away. It's only hard to access sometimes. Our critical brain tries to prevent us from feeling joy. After all, joy is risky. It is vulnerable. *If we get it, we may lose it.* Then, Responsibility takes over and says, *We must work. We mustn't play.*

When we tap into joy, we tap into something even deeper: Pleasure.

Seeking joy, finding joy, and knowing joy are not the same as worrying things will never be "good enough" or seeking unattainable perfection. Often, in the presence of joy, you'll find that they already are. Joy and pleasure bring you home.

Even when you're unsure, you can rest in what you do know: yourself. At the very least, you're becoming more known.

These five Radical Beliefs will help you get there. They won't solve every problem. They can't cure what plagues us, but they have the power to take you out of doubt. Combined, they tell their own tale:

I'm only ever doing the best I can.

I'm not trying to screw up my life.

This is all that exists now.

It's OK to be different.

Joy is my birthright.

Let these settle on your heart, and notice what happens to your body when you say them. Let them wrap around you when you need moral support. Take them. Rearrange them. Use them as you see fit. They're yours, after all.

As hard as it is to look back on my past, to see the mistakes that piled up faster than the laundry, I also can recognize now that they brought me to this place. This space is where I can roam and be free.

This land where there's room to breathe.

This land where we can follow more than one way.

Signposts aren't pointing to a single road.

We have many paths we can take.

And most importantly, we get to travel at our own pace.

I want you to meet this land. It's waiting for you, too.

Consider This:
- When have you had to put down the pursuit of a goal?
- What would that look like for you to put *best to rest*?

11

Get Comfortable With the Tension

I know what will happen if I don't change,
I don't know what can happen if I do.

U tilizing trauma-informed practices and understanding we can't do it all, we can get out of the boiler room and come up for air. It's possible for us to do it a new way when we learn a new way.

Looking back at that mid-Autumn day in 2020 when I broke at the table, it feels as if I went from out to in seamlessly, but in reality, there were many steps that took me from boarded and shuttered to open and trusting. Soon after messaging my friend, I took the second, biggest step I'd ever have to take: I set down my work to focus on my health. Similar to a decade prior, the new therapy I'd been waitlisted for was finally approved. It gave me hope for the first time in a year. Tangible support was on its way. I started sessions a few weeks later.

I also decided to finally try medication. I was willing to do whatever it took to regain my health.

After these two big changes to my life, color returned to my days. I saw and appreciated the changing of seasons. They no longer felt like time was mocking me, but rather became an invitation to rest along with them.

I held my family tighter, too. While I still had a long way to go to regain my partner's trust and settle myself into this new pace of living, I was finally able to set down the weight I'd been carrying. Much of that, of course, with the help of my therapist.

It wasn't easy to walk away from all that I was trying to build, but I finally gave myself permission to do so. I was learning, although I didn't know it at the time, that I could trust that life would be OK if I paused.

And in this pause, the greatest reformation began.

In many ways, it's still ongoing.

I didn't magically get better overnight. Not in 2014, not in 2018, not in 2022. Each breakdown required its own recovery. But each one started with small steps. Each one started with one step. And I get it. It can be increasingly frustrating to know that you have to be the one to put the work in. It can be further defeating to *know* the answers—the strategies, the way forward—but be unable to do it.

Just because it's simple doesn't mean it's easy. However, just because it's difficult doesn't mean it's impossible. In fact, as contrary as it may seem to have Radical Beliefs—we're looking for *subtle shifts* over *sweeping changes*. This is where our first PATH from Chapter One can help us. In our moment of tension, we can pause, breathe, and then ask ourselves what's really going on. We can think about what we need and remember we're only human.

Here's the chapter I wish I could write:

There's going to be tension.
We can learn to live with it.
/END.

And then, you're like, *Cool! Great! Thanks!* And everyone gets on with their day because our rational brains understand this is a fact of life.

But this is more like it:

There's going to be tension.
We can learn to live with it.
WAIT! Why is this so hard again?!

In fact, here's an actual journal entry I wrote as I was writing this chapter:

"I feel crappy. Anxious. Moody. Annoyed. I hate this. I hate how my "good" feeling went away. I worked so hard for it, and now it's gone. Everything feels dumpy." DOUBLE-YOU TEE EFF.

I've been writing some version of this for nearly twenty years. The day before I penned that journal entry, my general practitioner and I even had a call to discuss my medication. He asked, *"On a scale from 1-10, one being the lowest and ten being the best, how would you rate your mood over the last two weeks?"* I said, *"8... 9... honestly, I've been feeling really good lately."* And that was the truth.

And yet, in my journal the next day, I wrote that it was all slipping away.

Stunned, *again.*

Even as I wrote this, a greater knowing washed over me. *"Feelings are fleeing,"* I wrote. And they are. And yet, they take us on such a ride. Often, ones we never bought tickets for! So, how do we do it? How do we take solace *in this knowing* and not panic-away our life—the life we've been working so hard to build?

How do we reconnect after heartbreak? After getting burned? When the world feels too hot to touch? How do we keep living when we don't want to walk around with oven mitts?

That was when it dawned on me that I couldn't write this chapter how I'd like to. The *ideal.* Because we don't live there. We're not robotic. We do not input "tension" and automatically output "acceptance." It takes work to get there. And, however much our rational brains know that tension is difficult, it still kind of sucks to feel.

But… (and this is a big but)… it doesn't have to suck the life out of us.

Let me show you what I mean by that. How we can, in fact, live with and through the tension. Even when it pricks, prods, and pokes its way into us. We can learn to keep going.

Life, grief, hardship, and pain will all come to us eventually—we can't bypass it—and we can't assume we know how it will affect us. Most importantly, no matter our spiritual or emotional health, we are not above it.

Yet, we *can* carry on.

Moreover, there are things we can do now that maybe, just maybe, can soften the blow.

Maybe the other shoe will never drop, but if it does—before it does—we can pack our *emotional-emergency bag,* the things, people, comforts, and support we would need if our mental or physical state suddenly dipped. In this chapter, I share a few of mine.

It won't take away our heartbreak, but it will hold us while we're there.

Over the past few years, alongside my grief, during the drives I'd made across town, saddened by all that felt out of reach, I also learned resilience. Only, I didn't realize that's what was happening. At this point, it still felt like a daily slog, the skate through mud.

I wasn't sleeping well. I was overeating and using food to cope with my unsettled heart. I tried to exercise, but I didn't really have the time. We had no village to pass off the kids to. I'd try to fit in runs after they went to bed. But those became fewer and far between. I'd still wake every morning with a pit of misery.

Or so I thought.

This period, the hardest of my life, truly taught me what it meant to be resilient. But I didn't learn it overnight. It was painstaking day after painstaking day, often doing one single thing I could to hold on. When I think about it now, it was first a resistance, then a revolution, and lastly, a building up of much-needed resilience.

That's when I started my *Trackers*, as I affectionately call them. I drew what felt like battle lines in my notebook. I slid my flair tip pen from left to right and top to bottom to create tiny boxes. I made a grid ten columns wide and seven rows deep. This was going to hold me for the next 70 days.

My goal was to color in one box each day, preferably in the morning, as a way to set intention and show up for myself. I wasn't sure if I could do it, but I needed the accountability. I needed a place to check in with myself daily. Mostly, I just wanted to start feeling better.

It became like a promise to myself. I wrote what I hoped to see after the 70 days: *I want to be rested, content, and healthy by building muscles of letting go, and realizing I can take the pressure off myself so I can build community and exercise.*

It was a mouthful. But I realized there were habits I wanted to change. I needed sleep, less excessive snacking after 8 pm, and breakfast in the morning. Those were some physical needs, but I also had emotional goals. I wanted to see myself as worthy, beautiful, and human. I wanted to discern and evaluate my time and energy.

And I realized that in order to do that, I needed discipline. I conveniently reminded myself, "I" am in the middle of "discipline." So, in order for me to have the discipline to monitor my actions, especially around my time and energy, I had to ask myself, *"Does this serve my purpose?"* I didn't realize it at the time, but I believe this laid the groundwork for future-me to really be able to say "no" to some things in order for me to say "yes" to others. This book came from one of those "no's."

Each morning, I used my highlighters to fill in the new day, choosing a color based on my mood. Blue became peace, green signaled trust, peach was calm, yellow was inner light, and purple embodied my exploding spirit. Every morning, as part of my writing routine, I opened my journal and shaded in the next box. Soon, two boxes became ten. Eventually, ten turned to 20, and before I knew it, I was already to fifty, over halfway done. I could feel my mood improving.

On the outside, all I was really changing was watching what I ate at night. In my grief, exhaustion, and sometimes rage after the kids' bedtime, I'd turned to food to cope with all I didn't have. I wasn't eating for pleasure, I was eating to numb, to fill a void. To stuff myself with all that life couldn't offer. Adding to the fact my body felt stiff and uncomfortable, I knew I had to make a physical change first. This was in my control.

As the rainbow boxes compiled, I felt a comfort I hadn't experienced in a long time. *I was making progress.* I was doing this for myself.

I began this tracker two months after the Cobb Elementary massacre in Uvalde, Texas. For as much that had happened that year, this event broke me. Two months later, I still felt as depleted as the day I read that horrifying headline. As hard as it was to change, I knew nothing would get better if I didn't.

Being honest with myself about how sad and grieved I felt was the first step in this recovery. After this shooting, I felt like I lost a part of myself. All the years of school shootings, all the anti-Asian and Black hate, all the political show-downs, all the fighting, anguish, and anger blew up inside of me until I felt nothing. What had been in me swirling around became lead. I felt heavy and expressionless. I got through my days because I had to, but they were slow and arduous.

But then, one day, when I least expected it, something happened. I became less aggravated. I noticed the sun. I saw a bud. Something was different, but I couldn't quite figure out what it was yet. Then I got a thought I hadn't had in a very long time: *"Maybe I can try this... Just this. Not all the things. Not every day. Not all of the time. But just this, for this one moment."*

And I tried that and I saw that it worked. It gave me a genuine joy I hadn't felt in a long time. The next day, I tried again. Skeptical, but with more motivation:. *Could this be it? Could this be the moment things start to change...?*

Yes.

And then I was back into the realm of choice. I was free once again. As Echart Tolle says, "Nobody chooses dysfunction."[72] I did not choose grief and heartache, just like you didn't. You and I were not wrong for having these very human reactions to tragedy and defeat.

Besides, it's nearly impossible to see you have a choice when you're navigating heartbreak and depression, anxiety and turmoil. Choice does not feel like an option when you've reached those depths. Those choices can go run off a cliff for all we care because it's just not that easy.

But on this day, in that moment, it became a little more so.

Sometimes, it's also helpful to remind ourselves that we're likely already on the road. We can go at our own pace. And I get it. That feels dicey when we've manipulated ourselves into believing everything must happen in a heartbeat.

"Why can't I just know it all already?" we often bemoan.

I found myself with these thoughts again one late-summer morning in 2022.

Staring at my notebook, with the sun barely peeking through the windows, my fuse was already lit. I had started a new habit tracker a few days before this. But I was still stuck in the swirl of everyday tension and defeat. Each morning still felt like a struggle. At first, I worried this tracker would be useless. *How can I seriously still feel like this?* I wondered. *I just woke up!*

The process of learning was overwhelming.

And then one morning, as gentle as the morning light that filtered through the shades, I realized *I don't have to keep fighting this. This is where I am right now. I'm going to let it be.* And then things began to flow.

In this flowing out, in honoring where I was, I took time to recognize my regular rhythm, however undesirable it was:

Wake up before everyone else. Get restless with the thought the kids would wake up early and take away my quiet alone time. Fill with dread over whatever was unresolved in my life. Fill with deeper anguish over what was happening in the outside world. Feel useless, angry, and despondent.

But I kept on.

And in doing this, I cleared the path of resistance.

By truly acknowledging my thoughts and pausing to figure out what my body was trying to tell me, I turned another corner. By honoring the resistance and trusting the process, I was granted a reset.

While I hated having this swirl of emotion and tension lodged in me each day, I was trying to get more comfortable with it. One day, I even remembered one of my favorite quotes by writer, speaker, and spiritual director Marianne Williamson. She writes, "Ego says, 'I'll have peace when everything is in place. Spirit says, 'Have peace, and everything will fall in place.'"

Remembering those words, I eased. I softened.

In that moment, I remembered I had what it takes to keep going. To keep holding this tension. To be strong enough to let it go. And that I'm made in the waiting.

I once wrote:

Are we made in the waiting?
Or does the waiting make us?
Does the waiting weigh us?
Where do we go to wait?

Maybe we just go right *here.*

When learning something new, it can feel excruciating to be stuck in the "not there yet" liminal space I mentioned in the last chapter—the cognitive dissonance of knowing where you want to be and recognizing where you are. I've experienced that time and time again. Yet, it's genuinely the space where change occurs.

Change creates momentum. Momentum creates change. And another way for us to take those wobbly first steps into something new is by asking the right questions.

Let's start with the question that perplexed me for half a decade. And, I believe, at some point, one you've wrestled with, too. *Do I stay or do I go?*

The question I was most often asked since leaving the classroom is if I would return to the classroom. For the first year, it felt as ridiculous as asking someone who was just pulled out of raging waters if they wanted to go back in. *"Can't you see I'm on dry land now?! Keep that water away from me!"*

Later, the discouragement inside my heart said, *"Why does education have to be the only thing I do? Is that really all people see?"*

Of course, I knew their questions were well-intentioned. And they were most often made as part of small talk and ice-breakers. But I couldn't help but hear the White Christmas refrain, "What can you do with a general when he stops being a general?"[73]

I mean, what *does* a teacher do when she stops being a teacher?

(She talks about it, of course. *wink*)

Even as I wrote the majority of this manuscript, I wasn't sure I would return to the classroom. I still didn't have that answer or outcome worked out. I knew I was closer than when I had left. I also knew the only way I could return was by *living* what's outlined in this book.

I knew it would take more than pedagogical knowledge for me to reenter the classroom. I feared returning with the stale version of who I used to be. There's been too much grief, tension, longing, racial and political reckoning, and loss to go back to exactly what I was doing before. But it's nuanced, right? Because while we teeter with who we are now, we don't need to abandon who we were before.

Now, in this finished version, the published version you are reading right now, my circumstances have changed. I have changed. *This work* has changed me. I recognize that we can want to do better, learn more, AND be just as good with where we're at.

We can ask ourselves questions that get us closer to what's really on our heart. And I get it. It can be difficult and scary. Because what if we get an answer we don't want to hear? What if it's not *part of our plan*?

It's helpful to know that you can use a framework of questions to meet your season of need. For me, one powerful framework has been:

Ask the questions.

Meet your fears.

Be courageous.

These three sentences have long been a guiding statement for me. "Ask, Meet, Be" has become how I notice and care about my place in the world, whether that's personal and private or among community and society at large. It's given me perspective to realize that change is always possible. It's how willing and ready we are to make it happen.

"Ask, Meet, Be" was a springboard for me to begin sharing my writing publicly. The process of identifying what was scary to me made me come to realize we are all people with fears.

But we can still do hard things. This mantra became a way of life throughout my five-plus years of alcohol-free living. It also helped me to question my relationship with privilege and to see my place in our world of white supremacy. And it's helping me again, now, as I write this book. We will always have things we are scared of doing. There will always be something in us telling us to *just be grateful,* but friend, dear one, I know there's more inside of you. I know you're waiting to come out, too. "Ask, Meet, Be" can help you get there.

When facing uncertainty or desiring a change, I first ask myself a variety of questions for clarification. These might include: *What do you really want? If time or money weren't an obstacle, what would you choose? Why are you seeking this change?* Then, I turn my questions over to my fears. These often revolve around "what ifs." *What if I'm wrong? What if others disagree with me? What will they think?* I allow myself to hear what I'm afraid of. I "meet" these fears. I come to see they're just fears, not a life sentence. Or, as Brené Brown says, they're a story I'm telling myself based on past hurts.[74] Once I acknowledge these fears, I remind myself there can always be change. Lastly, I turn towards courage. *I have the power to make this change.*

To take this back to school, it may begin, for example, by noticing that you want to propose a new initiative in a staff meeting. You are passionate about a particular method and have done your research into its effectiveness. You really want to try this out, but you're worried about making waves. Just thinking about everyone staring at you with flat expressions makes your palms sweaty. You begin to hear your fears: *What if you fumble over your words? What if everyone thinks you don't know what you're talking about? What if you're wrong about this method?*

These fears make you want to hold back. But then you remember, they're just fears. It's OK to notice them. Doing so allows you to hold your humanity. You may even remember the "Radical Beliefs" from the last chapter—*You're not trying to mess up your life. It's OK to be different.*

At this point, you realize that *not* bringing it up would only be a disservice to you and others. Maybe it won't be accepted, but at least you'd have tried! *"I know what will happen if I don't change. I don't know what can happen if I do."* You're more curious about the unknown. You decide to move forward.

Ask the questions. Meet your fears. Be courageous.

With frameworks like the one above, I created a new life for myself. I came to see what wasn't helping me and discarded it. In its place, I picked up the things, habits, and people who were aligned with supporting the version of me I wanted to become.

If I stayed on the course I was at, I realized that was as far as my life was going to go. If I wanted to see something different, then I would need to act differently. I would need to change. This grew more out of curiosity about a different way of living, a different way of being. If I wanted a new life, then a rebirth was necessary.

Yet, what I realized is that we don't relapse because we are bad people; we relapse because we are hurting people; we are painful people. We relapse because we didn't have the tools to access our greatness in that moment, not because our greatness doesn't exist.

Whether inside the classroom or out, or during periods of questioning myself or waiting for answers, I had to forgive my mistakes so I could breathe again.

I had to see that I was still a worthy person underneath my cracked shell. I had to recognize what was and wasn't in my control, what I could and couldn't control.

A poem I heard in a sobriety meeting layered my perspective once again.

In a poem from her book, *There's a Hole in My Sidewalk*, Portia Nelson writes about the holes we fall into and if we go around them the next time.[75] This was read to me in a sobriety meeting from The Luckiest Club, a support group I joined during the pandemic.[76] While Portia Nelson's poem isn't necessarily about sobriety—at least not to my knowledge—it lends itself to the feeling of overwhelm. To the cycle of trying and failing and trying again. And, eventually, if we're aware enough, *consciousness. Newness. Something different.*

One day last year, this poem became reality.

I picked up my daughters from kindergarten. It was the first warm day of Spring. I decided to celebrate the moment with a surprise treat. We made the short walk from their school to the smoothie shop. Everything was heavenly until it wasn't! She didn't want to leave. She wasn't *ready* to leave. I gave reminders, but she ignored them. I gave redirections, and she started to talk back. Before I knew it, we were having a conversation about straws. Straws. Really? Is this really about straws?

Soon, her tears came. They gave way to the cacophonous whining and the wail heard 'round the world. The pit started to form in my stomach, the way it had so many times before. I looked to her sister, her twin, who I also had to find a way to get home. *Would she start too?* My fingers curled into their familiar position. My chest tightened.

I wanted to go in hard with the "This was supposed to be fun. You weren't supposed to get upset about this. *Ughhhh, why is this happening??!?!*"

I wanted to wail.

Inside my head, the chorus of regret began to play: "*Ugh, this was a mistake. Ugh, why did I think this would be a good idea?!? Ugh, ugh, ugh, ugh, ugh.*"

In that moment, I wanted to scream with her. We were finally out of the store, but the distance from store to home felt like a wilderness trail.

I had a brief moment to think—a miraculous moment, actually. "*Something has to change. Something that I don't really want to do needs to be done.*" And I did it. I asked her if she wanted a piggyback ride. It changed her mood, and we found a way to make it work. Did my other daughter start to complain a bit? Yes. But we had to find a way.

And it worked for a bit. And then it got a little sketchy again. But at that moment, when I was ready to ramp back up with the negative self-talk when I was ready to grade my parenting with a bold "F" for the zillionth time, I said, "No, Christina, actually, you just made a mistake. That's all this was. You're learning, too. It's ok. It's going to be ok."

Maybe I am sharing this because while I think it's so obvious, maybe it's not. It wasn't always so obvious to me because I was so mad at that moment. I was so mad it wasn't going how I wanted it to. I was so mad that my plan wasn't working. I'm a teacher; MY PLANS ARE SUPPOSED TO WORK. I DON'T MAKE PLANS THAT FAIL. I MAKE PLANS THAT ARE SUPPOSED TO BE GREAT. I'M A GREAT PLANNER. I LOVE PLANNERS. I LOVE PLANNING.

But why am I not so good at it anymore?!?!? This constant thought I heard frequently over the last few years.

But at that moment, it didn't matter. At that moment, I looked up at the sky and realized how small of a problem this was. It wasn't a life sentence. It wasn't a verdict. It was just me and my two daughters after a long day at school. It was an appropriate amount of disappointment for a drowsy child, and that didn't make me a bad mom (or a bad planner).

Maybe I can't remember this all the time, but I could do it for this one. And this one matters. Maybe I won't remember this the next time my own disappointment creeps in, but I don't have to because I didn't need to think about *those* moments during this one. I just had to focus on the present. In fact, if I did try to think about my success rate for all future meltdowns as this one was happening, what would happen is what *has happened* in the past—nothing.

Well, not nothing. Increased heart rate, balled fists, and my own rising temperature. That's what. If I tried to think about my success in every possible future tantrum, I'd stall. It'd be too overwhelming. I know this because I've tried. Many times, in fact. And that's what made that moment so special. I saw a different way. I chose a different path. A chronic negative self-talker who is prone to perfectionism and rumination had enough awareness to give grace in the moment. And what a difference it made.

That day in the park, under the spring sky, I tried again. I tried a new way. I went around the hole versus falling in. I walked down a new street.[77]

Will I spot the next one before I plummet? I don't know. God willing, yes, but that's not the point. I don't have to worry about that one right now. I can take solace in this small but mighty victory. In her oft-quoted words, Laura McKowen reminds, "I can push off from here."

And that's what we can do here, in the classroom. We can push off from here. It's not about doing it better; it's about doing it differently. We can't operate the way we used to. Doing things differently isn't asking for more from us; it's actually asking for less. But initially, it does require awareness. It requires some discipline. But more than anything, it requires grace. Because we won't always hit the mark. Sometimes, we will knock it out of the park—we'll remember our tools, keep our cool, and move on with peace. But for so many other moments, we'll slip. We'll fall. We'll stumble our way to the next signpost. And that's OK, too. This is OK. Because we're trying. We're trying on something new for us. Grace and self-compassion won't come naturally when you've spent decades berating yourself for your mistakes. But they will come with practice. And that's what this is.

It's exchanging what we thought we needed in the classroom and replacing it with something that's quite simpler. We need a way to be kinder to ourselves when life doesn't go according to plan, when the student yells in our face, when the parent wants us fired, when our colleague drives us mad, when you ran out of time, when the project didn't get finished, when that student didn't reach the next level, when our spouse feels distant, our children disappoint us, or health scares abound. We must find a way to make it through the intensity of living an uncontrollable life.

Teachers work in the people business. A classroom becomes an organism in itself. So many processes, so many parts. For the longest time, I thought I could control it all. I thought it was my job to control it all. I see now I can't—let alone that I don't *want* to control it all! Can I help establish order and community? Absolutely. But can I do that without the high stakes of believing I have to perform beyond my human level? Well, that's what this work is, after all.

I can't operate there anymore. And I want to help you see that you do not need to either. You can set down some of those bags you've been carrying. I know they've been heavy. Instead, I want you—I want *us*—to be able to pick up peace where we can, when we can. It won't be all of the time. We have peace until we don't have peace, and then we have peace until we don't. *Impermanence.*

It's OK if it doesn't always feel good. That's not the point, either. As much as my young 20-something self loved to believe, I am not a person who can stand on peace alone. But I can equip myself with the skills and strategies, the tools, and the teachers who help me see I am not alone. I can fill myself with the love that gives me a new voice. One that says I don't have to be perfect to still be good. This is the hallmark of grace and self-compassion, the pieces I can collect to move me forward. These are the bags I wish to carry.

On we go.

You're going to be alright, teacher. You're going to figure this out. With grace, with patience, and with compassion, you've got this. And it's OK if it takes time. This is not a race. Keep going in the direction of you.

There can always be change.

Consider This:

- Recall PATH 1 invites us to **P**ause, **A**sk ourselves, "What's really going on?", **T**hink about what we need, and **H**old on to our humanity. Picture yourself using this in a moment of tension or resistance. What does that look like? What does that sound like?

- *Ask, Meet, Be* helps us determine what changes we seek and what fears get in our way. Combine this framework with the accountability methods you respond well to (e.g., *Trackers*, social group, calling a friend) to support you in the next change you wish to make.

12

Recognize You Have So Much to Offer

May that be possible for me, too.

You've made it this far. You can keep going.

You may not always have the fight in you, but you will always be enough. Your bad days do not define you any more than the praise you receive for your productivity.

We don't give ourselves enough credit for the burdens we carry. Not as teachers. Not as individuals. And teacher, you've been carrying so much. It's OK to let it down. It's OK to let it out. And if that resistance is there, if it's still clinging in knots to your insides, please know it won't be there forever. You will come to a place where you will see that you are more than any of your bad days. You've always been more. We have been dealt a lot, and yet, there are things we can still do to make this *work* work for us.

Growing self-compassion, grace, and patience allows us to do what matters to us.

You're not ignoring how hard this work is or the circumstances pressing at our palms. You understand that since the beginning of formal teacher preparation, the odds have been stacked against us. And the burdens only seem to get heavier. Yet, we don't need to condone policies to still be able to teach within them. Instead, we can recognize and call them out. They can exist, **and** we can be upset about it. Perhaps our anger will lead us to what's really on our hearts.

Even in my lighter mood and better health, I often find myself waiting for the other shoe to drop. But what if it never drops? Or, what if we're better apt to handle it when it does? To know that we can get through the tough times again.

Maybe it's OK if living things break down because they can also rebuild. *"Is this maturity?"* I ask myself. Maybe, maybe not. But it is something. It's carrying on when we live in unpredictable quarters.

Because what if, notwithstanding what is out of our control, we didn't have to feel so panicked? What if the tension was something we could learn to live through?

What if we saw it as regular as breathing?

As life-changing as the passing of seasons?

What if we simply became comfortable with it?

I want to lead you there. Not because I've become impervious—not because I can maneuver tension flawlessly—but because I know what happens when we let it fester. When we ignore it or when we act on it impulsively.

But let me be clear: This is not about avoiding the tension. It's about understanding that while this conflict cannot be controlled, it can be noticed. Once noticed, we can get to work.

Because we get to choose how we show up.

If not, Tension will have a heyday.

And I don't know about you, but I'm kinda ready for "Yay-Days." Or, maybe we should say, "Bey-Days." You have so much to offer, my friend. We're headed there next.

Remember those Beyoncé days? We started the book with them. If you forgot, that's OK. Understandably, with all that we've uncovered with Teacherhood they may be a faint memory. But you didn't come this far *not* to shine! We're not learning self-compassion, grace, and patience to stay dull. We're allowing it to ignite us once again. To live freely, openly, and with ease in our bodies. We're coming home.

And that starts by identifying what's trying to keep us estranged.

Remember when Kanye grabbed the mic from Taylor Swift at the 2009 VMAs? Our "inner saboteur," as RuPaul loves to call our inner critic, is Kanye at that moment. Our inner saboteur wants to take our moment of glory and crumble it between his fingers. He wants to shout and tell us we don't deserve recognition. *Someone else is doing it better.*

And, unfortunately, we try to please, so we stand there a little stunned and *just take it*. We walk off stage believing that we're not worthy of love. We doubt our skills. And, without ever realizing it, we turn off our lights.

Now, what do you think Beyoncé would have done?

(For the record, this is not a B vs T match, but stick with me...)

KANYE WOULDN'T HAVE STOOD A CHANCE.

Bey would've shut it down.

She knows who she is!

She's not going to let a lowly voice turn off her light.

(And frankly, neither did Tay. Um, hello, 2023 tour.)

In all reality, I'm sure Beyoncé *does* hear the voice of her inner critic (we all do), but she's learned how to persevere.

Guess what? We're gonna be like Bey.

But first, let's turn to the other Queen B.

Brené Brown famously says you don't get to be the critic if you're not in the arena. Guess what? Our inner saboteur isn't in the arena. You are! This is your permission to silence it as needed. Because sometimes it's just mean. And we don't need that! No, thank you!

And… (and this is a big "and")…

Sometimes, it's worth listening to it if only to hear what it has to say.

When I took time to hear what mine had to say, over-whelmingly, it whispered I wasn't good enough. I would never be good enough. I had to keep striving. And, often, because of envy, I felt threatened anytime someone else's light shone. I couldn't see their victory as a win for us all; I could only see them doing better than me. The critic in my head told me that even if I succeeded, I'd be a copier (thanks to middle school conditioning). *No bueno.*

Unfortunately, that experience of accusing my coworkers early in my career wasn't the last time I got tangled in my own thinking. Nor was it the last time I felt jealousy towards a colleague or teacher-friend. You name it, I felt it: Bigger, cleaner classroom. *Check.* Good relationship with families. *Check.* More socially connected. *Yep.* Professional Development Advancement. *Oh yeah.* And don't get me started on all the ways social media has induced confidence-comas!

On my hard days, I couldn't see that my biggest competitor wasn't another teacher or parent; it was myself. On top of that, I couldn't see the good right in front of me when some-one else was glowing beside me. I lived in my own hell of scarcity and never knew it.[78] I was constantly in competition with others, but also, really, in competition with myself. And my inner critic always let me know I was down.

Worse, this competition between myself and others edged me further away from connecting with those when I needed it the most. Being honest about my troubles was difficult when I didn't want to appear weak or unknowledgeable. And I did not want pity. My pride and shame buried me. And, if I'm being honest, I didn't want help—at least my ego didn't. My ego really just wanted to find a way to solve it all on my own. But, at the time, I couldn't even say that because that would have made me unknowing *and* self-centered, arrogant *and* needy. Instead, I shoved my need and shame deeper and vowed to solve it myself.

From scarcity to imposter syndrome, these moments showed me how much self-compassion, grace, and patience are needed.

If you had come around my house anytime in Winter 2023, you'd have heard a particular battle cry from my daughter. *Nothing was fair! She never got what she wanted!* Meanwhile, fed up with my inability to reach her, I just wanted to scream back, "LIFE ISN'T FAIR." But that wouldn't have helped her situation. She felt someone else, her twin sister, in this case, had it better than her.

I tried to tell her I understood. Because I really did.

For high-striving individuals like you and me, it's hard not to want to be the best. And it becomes our Achilles heel. The competition we create between us and our colleagues, friends, or other parents pushes away the very people who know exactly what it takes to do this work.

Specifically, it creates resentment. This has happened to me in every work setting. And it was only when I learned how to better identify this feeling that I had a chance to move on from it.

Throughout my career and early parenthood, including my attempt at homeschooling and pivoting to writing, the resentment and rumination ship was always coming and going. Coupled with my desire to seek "enlightenment" or reach for the "best" way to do something, I'd obsess over details. If something didn't work, I couldn't easily let it go. I wanted to know why it broke down and how I could fix it.

Usually, that meant obsessing over every single detail in my head until I could figure out what went wrong. If I could pinpoint it, I'd be able to fix it next time. If I could pinpoint it, I wouldn't repeat this mistake. If I could pinpoint it, maybe the mistake wouldn't be there.

However, it never occurred to me that many times when I thought I was being reflective, I was ruminating. For many years, I saw my reflection practices as a strength. And, for sure, they were! But I didn't know that those nights I laid in bed and churned and crunched over my actions, I was sabotaging myself. I couldn't see that my endless replaying of details wasn't producing any new outcomes. Instead, I became increasingly anxious, frustrated, angry, and sad.

When I was actively teaching, I often applauded myself on my reflective nature and ability to assess situations or lessons. It helped me be a more effective educator, and in my personal life, it felt like it kept me on track. But when my inner critic went off again over these past few years, all this back-and-forth confused me about my strengths. Then, I happened upon a tool that gave me a new perspective.

One tool that has drastically changed my point of view on my strengths and weaknesses is the Enneagram. It's an ancient tool used to highlight our motivations for our behaviors.[79] It's a system of nine interconnected personality types that showcase what we think, feel, and do.[80] While an individual will have parts of each type, they will often identify most with one particular number. I share many of the same motivations, stressors, and behaviors as Type One "The Reformer." Other types, or numbers, include such traits as "The Helper" or "The Peacemaker," types Two and Nine respectively. You can find your type by taking a quick internet quiz and by learning from those who have studied the Enneagram in depth.

As a guest on "The Next Right Thing" podcast, Enneagram scholar Suzanne Stabile taught me this: "Your strengths are also your weaknesses."[81]

What serves you well can also hurt you. When held too tightly, you lose the good, and the bad overwhelms. And that's what was happening. I could see it all so clearly. Whenever I spoke too harshly about my choices or wallowed in self-doubt, my inner critic told me I was all bad. All wrong.

One thing that makes me a great teacher *is* my ability to reflect, assess, and pivot. I can ask myself the difficult questions and use my inner compass to point to the right, to the just. But left unchecked, and it all goes sideways. When regret and guilt nag on my conscience, those same motivations cause me to spiral. To snowball. To think of every possible thing wrong. I become my worst critic. My strengths become my downfall. And it's hard to lead your class when you're depleted.

Just like children need a social-emotional guide, so do the adults who teach them.

It is very difficult to be around others when you feel a constant lack. The Enneagram knowledge I've gained has also helped me to see I'm not alone. When I learned that other Enneagram Ones, "The Reformers," also feel the compulsion to make the world the best it can be, it allowed me to breathe. It allowed me to see this is part of who I am.

When I first learned about burnout, I didn't think I was burned out, but when I finally had a word to label my experience, I felt so seen and validated. I didn't feel like a singular failure. The same thing was happening here. I understood it more clearly. Once I could describe this inner drive and recognize that so many others feel it too, I felt less alone. I could do something about it. It's not a personality flaw; it's a trait. It helped me to accept who I am. Learning that others have a loud inner critic gave me more compassion for my trying heart.

When my postpartum intake counselor first mentioned I struggled with perfectionism, I was angry. I didn't want to wait to get better. I wanted to get better instantly. I was in the "Lost Souls Room," a death for the dead, that eerie hallway in Beetlejuice where Barbara and Adam pull up the window shade to reveal ghoulish figures floating around.[82] I was haunted with new thoughts.

Where am I?
Where do I go from here?
My whole life feels like a lie now.
Anything I thought was a strength was actually perfectionism in disguise. Cool. Great.
Am I even good at anything?
Was I ever a good teacher?
Will I ever get rid of this?

I wanted to fight.
I wanted to push.
I wanted to kick, beat, and blast this thing away.
I wanted to *scream.*

Incidentally, writing this book has opened up new avenues for learning. Whether it was intentional research or answers that led to more questions, I unearthed a whole slew of information about myself during this process. I'm still processing some of that. Some of it has already informed what's been laid before you.

When I started this book, I thought I had to cut the cord on my striving. I thought all my striving might be the cause of what's been holding me back. This was the message I received from society. What I've learned about perfectionism while writing about perfectionism flipped me on my head *again*. I'm learning that this is part of who I am, not a stain I need to remove but an itch I must scratch.

The insights I've learned from Suzanne Stabile's Enneagram work, combined with Katherine Morgan Shaffler's words on perfectionism, have also helped me to realize that my "perfectionism" is both a strength and a weakness.

Through Shafler's writing and her appearance on "The Marie Forleo Podcast," she's helped me understand that perfectionists don't need everything to be perfect, nor are we looking for every single thing in our life to be square. Rather, our perfectionism comes out in the things that are *most important to us*.[83]

Can it negatively affect me? Has it negatively affected me? Absolutely. But it's also wholly, fully captivated me. It's made me exactly who I am. This book would not be here without this drive in me—the same drive I suspect you have, too. That's why when I talk about *replacing* your perfectionism for power, I don't mean to eliminate it, but rather to shift it around to meet your needs. Because yes, when not managed well, perfectionism can rear its ugly head. That's why your struggles have been so hard for you.

A vital point and uplifting perspective Shafler offers in her book, *The Perfectionist's Guide to Losing Control: A Path to Peace and Power*, is that we can take our struggles related to seeking perfection and turn them into challenges.[84] And the key is connection. Shafler writes that when you're supported, you no longer suffer in isolation but instead move toward a new version of yourself. She even goes so far as to say, "If you're struggling with your mental health, don't assume it's because there's something wrong with you; assume it's because you don't have the support you need." In her words, when you have support, your struggle becomes more of a challenge—something that can be met and overcome. Leveling up but without all the external validation required. Leveling up, but in a healthy way, from knowing and owning who you are.

Shafler's entire book is a clear message for all (perfectionists or not): Who you are is already worthy. You are already whole. Perfectionist or not, there is nothing about you that you need to get rid of. When we open ourselves to new ways of being, we gain compassion; in this case, for both the empowerment that comes from "being a perfectionist" and the struggle.

In 2019, after more transitions—and indefinite space away from the classroom—I realized I had lived my whole teaching life in fear. I had moments of love, but I hustled those. I was in a constant state of "not enough." Even when I thought I knew, I thought someone else knew more. I let my voice be little. One summer morning, not too long after that school year ended, I sat on my front patio with my coffee next to me, and in my journal, I wrote:

Today, I am going to show up and sing my heart. Because singing your heart is never a failure. And, doing what you love is not your ego talking. Fear is the ego. You let go of fear, you let go of ego. You let go of ego, you can do the true work.

I am going to show up today and not care if I fail. I am not even going to worry about that thinking as being detrimental. Because the truth is, when I care about me failing—it is just that. I care about me. I can't care about you if I am concerned about me. When I care about failing, I hold myself back.

I share this because this chapter is all about letting go. About having the freedom to change. And, most importantly, remembering who you are.

Love, you are the compassion, the grace, and the patience bundled into one.

You're magnetic.

With the watts and voltage to shine for days.

My world changed when I saw my potential formed in small bits on that summer patio. It's not always that we need to change, but we can. We have the potential. Love, I think you can light the way. You can do amazing things when you tackle what gets in your way. But you need to know what those things are.

Maybe it's the golden rays of the California coast seeped deeply into my soul, but the lessons I learned there, within my classroom, are shining through me and onto you right now.

When we play small, the world stays small

When we shine bright, the whole world gets light.

At some point, you're going to forget your light. You're going to forget how brightly you can shine. And I know the things on your heart are too great to be left in the dark.

We must be aware of what is happening in our minds. Your whole life can change based on what you think. While you can't control your thoughts, you can start to see they are there. You can begin to believe that what you think determines your outlook.

Learning self-compassion, grace, and patience is all about making the changes inside so we can do the work on the outside. It's about noticing what's outside can impact your inside. It's all about making you aware of yourself and your situations so that you can make necessary changes to benefit yourself and those around you. We need to recognize our own power before we can empower others. We need to transform ourselves so we can transform our teaching.

One way we can do that is by recognizing what gets us down.

Remember that arena? With all the naysayers and boo-ers? Remember that we're allowed to turn them off?

This is where we want to tune into what's really under our hurt. Not all voices in our head are a bad thing. By now, it's clear that having a healthy relationship with your thoughts can strengthen your mental wellness. But before we throw away every undesirable thought we have, we need to learn how to understand what they're saying.

In fact, sometimes even the "bad" thoughts can be a good thing.

Say hello again to Envy. (Ugh, I know! Does it make you feel icky and small and, generally, like a pretty resentful person, too? Well…)

Envy has the power to inform.

Envy allows you to see what is really important to you. It can also allow you to plan for things you know might dim your light.

One particular summer, when my meditation practice was on point, I took my journaling a step further. Maybe it was the anxiety-addled brain that needed an emergency plan, but either way, it gave me a roadmap for the inevitable bumps I'd experience throughout the upcoming school year. I thought back to my previous year and those before it and noted what situations tripped me up—which areas brought out the most comparison, envy, or irritation.

On the left side of a sheet of notebook paper, I wrote down what those included. For me, they were: others' beautiful classrooms, feeling out of control when students weren't listening, and not feeling like I was growing professionally, to name a few.

On the right side, across from each one, I wrote a corresponding affirmation for what I could tell myself when those thoughts cropped up, such as, "The grass is just as green on my side" or "I have strengths, too." It was a reminder for me that, one, these were things that were going to bother me, and two, I could have a plan and respond differently.

I looked at the internal pressures I struggled with: doubt, comparison, envy, and fear. For me, those showed up as repeatedly questioning my methods, fretting over someone else's room looking nicer than mine, growing bitterness if others were achieving or getting positions that I wanted, and ultimately, feeling like a failure at the end of the day. I didn't want to disappoint myself or the parents of the children I served.

By doing this, I had a plan of action when difficult scenarios arose.

Looking at what triggers me and planning for what to do next came to serve me again years later. One of the first mom groups I connected with online after we moved to Canada was created by illustrator and former teacher Jamina Bone, founder of MommingWithTruth.[85] Her work and illustrations often portray the tension and beauty of motherhood, all the while advocating for maternal mental health.

When we moved to Canada, I felt alone and overwhelmed. Like many modern-day moms, I turned to social media for affirmation and belonging. I appreciated the popular parenting social media accounts reflecting conscious, gentle parenting, but I still needed more. I needed someone who got the struggle. I needed someone who knew what it felt like to be down on your parenting. While Jamina's work always inspired and resonated with me, I formally met her by taking a leap of faith and joining the online membership she ran in Fall 2019. It was a small group of women scattered across the U.S., but we found solace and community instantly. We knew what it was like to have experienced postpartum anxiety, depression, general overwhelm, and disappointment in our motherhood experiences. And we also understood we wanted more and were willing to do what it took to get there. Her community met me right where I was, and I am forever grateful to her and the other moms—my sisters—who provided a place to land.

As time went on, Jamina would occasionally run a course and provide resources we could use that helped us reflect on our parenting. One particular resource was called a "Temperature Check," a simple yet effective way to review and plan for your week. Jamina's ability to understand what modern moms were experiencing allowed her to create tools for us to see our needs and desires. Another such tool was taking a quiz she created that helped me identify what kind of mother I was. Out of four possible options, I came away with "Seen and Heard." I felt so validated in discovering this part of me. Arguably, it was already becoming clear to me that I desired to be seen and heard, particularly in the growing bitterness I felt towards my husband at the time as we raised our twin toddlers.

Motherhood gave me an outlet and a new set of keys to explore parts of myself that had been hidden and tucked away for a long time. I believe teaching can help us explore our unmet needs as well. We're slammed with second-to-second decision-making and often teeter between caring for ourselves and caring for our students.

Examining the parts of Teacherhood that are both life-giving and undesirable can give us a new window into ourselves. In turn, it can also open doors for those around us. It can show us what gets in the way, what needs to stay, and what needs to go.

While journals remain my go-to form of connection to consciousness, after we moved to Canada, I became intimately acquainted with Google Docs and the Notes app on my phone. Just like with my old journals, I'll often go back through these folders to recount history and to see how much I've grown or just to remember what was happening at a particular time. Occasionally, and particularly around heightened seasons of grief, such as the summer of 2020, the words and emotions from those moments jump off the page. I remember the raw emotion so clearly.

In writing this chapter, I came across one such passage. I was surprised by my own grace and persistence to keep going when I couldn't see the road ahead:

What if my "moment" is sitting through the most uncomfortable part of the process? What if on the other side of this dark, grimy, murky, swamp-like water is resolve? What if the pasture is just beyond what I can't see?!

Can I just get in the boat?

Can I look around at all that is scary and know that my current is still moving? It's still taking me down the road, er, waters? However rough they may be. I am in my boat but those things can't get me. They are happening, yes, but they are not happening to me. *They are happening around me. If I can keep my boat straight. If I can wait this one out, I WILL get there.*

Can I be a witness to the bumps?
Can I be a witness to the shakes?
Can I be a witness to the dark?
Can I keep my boat afloat?

Yes. Yes, I can.

I can keep watching.
I can keep witnessing.

I can keep seeing the scary scenes play out. But they are not happening to me, they are just happening around me.

If I can stay in this boat, there are smoother, brighter waters ahead.

God, will you give me the strength to stay in the murky waters?

Will you give me the patience to wait this one out?

Will you help me to see all that I can be once I truly believe in myself?

Yes.

I was deep in FOMO and frustration of my "moment" passing me. I grieved what felt like the loss of my book idea and ability to help teachers—to be a writer and a stay-at-home-parent—and change the world.

But something inside me needed to change.

Perhaps it feels a bit easier to write this now because I see that I have achieved those goals in some ways, but what feels the most special to me is that I held on. Although I was still a year away from setting down the pressure to achieve something special with my life—particularly the book and changing the world—I am still amazed at the way Trust was beginning to form in my bones.

I was so scared of what putting down my goals would mean, but I also knew that I couldn't sustain myself if I continued to grip them.

That period taught me Patience on a level I had never understood before.

As high-strivers, it feels achingly hard to wait out when we've decided there's something we want to achieve. Or when we notice someone else getting it. When the dream calcifies in our heart, it's difficult to think of much else. And because it feels like this goal is in reach but not quite in our hands, the present moment lacks ease. We see how much further we have to go. We're not good enough yet. We're not *there*.

We put a metric ton of pressure on ourselves to perform. Society and social media influence how much we think we ought to achieve. In others' picture-perfect moments, it feels as if we have to have it all. We *should* have it all. We *could* have it all. All is up for grabs (if only we work a little harder). This absorbed message drips with the pressure to have all of our buckets full, all our plates spinning at the same time.

It's just not sustainable.

It's just not reality.

One day after dropping my kids off at school—and in the middle of writing this book—I felt that prickly presence of restlessness crawl through my body again. *I wasn't as far along as I should be.* The thought was so unspecific but crystal clear, one I've heard my whole adult life.

After drop-off, I made my way to a trail where I planned to exercise. I wanted to run. I wanted to keep up with my routine, my end goal of being fit enough again to run a 5K.

I didn't want to walk.

But I soon realized, on that particular day, I was too tired for the level of output a run would require. I settled on walking.

I walked half a mile with full force and speed. While it felt good to be outside, my *not-good-enough* thoughts still nagged at me. I kept on. The more I moved, I hoped, the more they would dissipate.

Then, with my lungs full of the fresh, brisk air and my legs asking for a break, I realized something. Even that pace was too much for me. As I listened to my body, I knew that all I really needed was movement. Not a push forward. Not a race to the finish line.

I slowed down. And everything came into view.

Maybe it doesn't need to be the fastest walk, but a walk.

Not the best life, but a life.

My body eased hearing these words. My shoulders lowered. I sank a little more steadily into the ground. I was part of the rhythm around me.

Spring came into focus. More words formed in my soul: *The best things are already around me.*

The squirrels played. The berries popped, and the faces of my family came into view. The purple crocuses pointed to the sky and invited me to their party.

I was in it.

I already have what I need.

I slowed, I stopped, I noticed some more.

I love who you are right now.

In that moment, I became who I was.

We get to decide what's important to us. We will have seasons where we work tremendously hard and want to epically change the world. This is practically written into our DNA, but we will also have other times when we need to retreat. We need to stay quiet. We need to quietly grow. Exist without the pressure to grow. *I love who you are right now.*

I can control the love I give to myself. I can't control how long the feeling will last. I can control if I try again. I can't always control what made it so difficult. I can say NO. I can say YES. I am captain and passenger. Steward and follower. Everything and nothing.

Like you, I can't control what tragedies befall us, what emotions swirl in those around us, or how seasons of life will wear on our bodies more than others, but I can see what those moments have to teach me.

I can keep listening even if I don't always like the words being said. I can keep my heart in the game even if I need to take a break. I can put down what doesn't serve me. I can pick up what does. I can carry on.

I recently wrote this note to myself, recognizing the growth I've made.

THANK YOU FOR NOT GIVING UP.

THANK YOU FOR NOT GIVING UP.

THANK YOU FOR NOT GIVING UP.

This is in our control. May you know this, too.

Consider This:

- Envy can help inform us of what's important to us. How has envy helped you determine what you want? How has it held you back?
- Make a list of what triggers you most at home and work. Write new words to tell yourself during those situations.

13

Choose What Gets You

Things will grow if we take the time to nurture them.

Sometimes, it gets lonely at the top. When you're stepping into your power and trying new things, that's when you'll hear the voices that try to pull you down. You'll hear the voice of doubt, worry, confusion, and hesitancy. Of, *Wait!* Or, *Not Now!*

But push, push, push, and do it anyway. Keep going, friend, because that voice is Kanye trying to grab the mic. Don't let him! Better yet, listen and move on. Because movement creates momentum. And momentum powers change. And even the desire to change can lead you to ask yourself the hard questions. The right questions. And we're about to get to asking.

We're about to find out what's been on your heart.

One of my most successful years in terms of the impact on my mental health was the year I started with a plan. A plan I worked out in the summer before school even started. As

I was doing this, I couldn't believe I had never thought to start the year by listing my goals. It made sense to me why I always reached but never quite felt accomplished. Why there was always a carrot but I could never catch it. When I started the year with a plan and gave priority to my life beyond the student curriculum, it gave me *intention*. It set my purpose for the year.

Tom and David Kelley, brothers and founders of the d. school at Stanford University and coauthors of *Creative Confidence: Unleashing the Creative Potential Within Us All*, believe the *intentionality* behind design thinkers—like Steve Jobs—is what brings them success. In their book, they write, "When [design thinkers] look around the world, they see opportunities to do things better and have a desire to change them." In short, we "improve on the status quo."[86]

And that's exactly what asking the right questions and choosing your path gets you. It sends us on a new trajectory to create a world that makes sense to us.

One shift I made during my time at Montessori School of Oakland completely changed my approach, and it had very little to do with instruction. Fed up with feeling stagnant and stale and as if I were an observer in my life rather than the main character, I started by scrawling down a basic credo: *I don't want work to take over my life*. I went on to write:

I want my life to be full of small moments that transform into a life well lived.

I do not want stress and anxiety, fear and hate, bitterness and loathing to take hold.

I want to enjoy my time.

Each day I have a choice to enjoy my time.

These five sentences sparked a whole new way of looking at the school year to come. I still have a photo of that notebook message saved on my phone. It became another turning point in my story.

Even though I wasn't sure what the year would bring, I felt a shift. For the first time, I felt mentally prepared to take on the year. This wasn't merely about setting up my classroom or getting the students' names prepared on materials; this was me taking control of my life and my health. This was proactive instead of reactive. This was me writing down common triggers and planning for their arrival. Thanks to years of steady journaling and looking inward, I was aware of what makes me tick in the classroom, so I created a plan to avoid future combustion.

Once again, being honest about where I was allowed me to walk a new path. What I hope you take away from the Paths offered in this book is that it's OK if they take some time. Understandably, we don't always *like* it when they take time, but taking time does not mean you're losing out. In fact, the opposite can happen. Funnily enough, my fingernails taught me that!

Being my mother's daughter means I'm a nail-biter. Our nails were often short, brittle, and damaged from hard work. But, like my mother, things started to change when I noticed them. For her, that meant going to the nail salon—the first thing I can ever recollect her doing for herself. Interestingly, it also became somewhat of a symbol of my mental health years later. If my nails were manicured and fresh, I was feeling fresh and energized. Fractured, short, and bare? Well, fractured, short, and bare.

Once, at the suggestion of my therapist, I did a little self-care for myself. I painted my nails. I didn't think much of it until a month later. I looked down and saw growth! Actual, factual growth! Here was my proof that things would grow if I nurtured them.

Not only did I have beautiful nails, but a new affirmation to guide me. In a journal, I wrote, *"Things will grow if we take the time to nurture them."*

By 2014, I'd racked up a half dozen college-ruled notebooks to capture my writing, but this leather-backed journal was different. My mother gifted it to me my senior year of high school, and I'd been waiting for the right time to use it. For the right words.

At 27 years old, with my nails painted cherry-red, I finally found them.

With its amber-gold palette and delicate design, it holds the affirmations and mantras I've amassed over the past decade. It retains my spirit in ink.

The moment those words landed on my soul in March 2014, I knew it marked a new beginning for me. I immediately wrote them down. This mantra reminds us that we do have power when we settle in patience.

The end goal is often a very important one, particularly if looking for a new position, but let's not underestimate the process itself. When done with care, it allows us to welcome a solution more easily.

It can also lead us to get specific about what we're trying to grow. Looking back at my own process, I realized that when you're in the midst of a problem and are looking for solutions, it's helpful to have a framework so you know the right kind of questions to ask and when.

Right now, you might be wondering, *Where do I even begin?* I've got you.

One particular evening, reflecting on my new bedtime routine of including meditation, I felt the warmth of pride and love. I was becoming who I wanted to be. I was beating the beast that started to grow within. And yet, I recognized I was in a brain fog of sorts. Lots was happening around me, but I didn't feel I had access or an exit. Everything around me moved, but I felt slow, stuck, and trapped—like in a shaken snow globe. Things got busy at home and work, and I stopped going to the gym. My husband and I were crisscrossing again. I wasn't keeping up with my practices. I didn't feel in a panic, but more like a coast. That night, I thought about an old skateboarding quote my husband used to say: "If you look good, you feel good. If you feel good, you skate good." It got me thinking. *When do I feel good? When do I feel best?*

And then, in that same affirmation journal, I wrote:

I feel best when I exercise.

I feel best when I meditate.

I feel best when I love.

I feel best when I am full.

These answers reminded me that in the hustle and bustle of life, I need very little to be content. Of course, I want purpose and belonging; I want social connections and fitness, but when it comes to feeling my best—what truly makes my heart sing, I need little. I need simple.

At the start of this book, I mentioned that we often neglect to attach our safety straps. We think we will go on unscathed. And while it's true that we can't protect ourselves from everything, we can choose to be proactive in our process to prepare for the inevitable hard days. It's Insurance 101, except rather than put money aside, we pack our bags for well-being. We ask ourselves what we need to feel better. We ask, *Who makes us feel better?* Other questions might include:

What's one thing I can do today to steady myself?

What brings me the most comfort?

Who can I talk to when things get hard?

What foods will nourish me?

This is preparing for an *emotional emergency*. While *Hot Cheetos* and *Pepsi* have their place, we want—and need—more when our ground crumbles even if it's a temporary rattle.

Having a plan for what we know will bother us—before the school year even starts—is one way to set yourself up for success. Because once we get into the problem, it takes a lot more than willpower to respond the way you'd like. In fact, we're more often than not reactive to our life events.

Asking the question, '*What makes me feel better?*' can also be achieved by simply asking, '*What do I need? What do I want?*' When life begins to feel overwhelming, and you realize you're just chaperoning your school bags from work to home without ever looking in them, and you're on your third night of take-out, and you can't even remember the last time you chose the gym over Netflix, knowing what you want and need can help break the cycle you are caught up in. *What's really going on here?*

I know that I've waited a little too long to ask those questions when it feels as if the water is just about to reach my nose. But those times will happen. We're human. Still, having an awareness of yourself, gained through stopping and questioning yourself, can provide the drainage you need.

Sometimes, the answer might surprise you. If you've been running around like a mad person, doing all the things for everyone else, and you ask yourself what you want, you may be taken aback to hear your inner self shout back: ALONE TIME! Or, what I often hear: *I just need my kids away from me, and I need quiet time, and I don't want anyone to bother me!* I'm surprised by how quickly I had an answer once I asked. But that's the thing: we have to ask, or else we continue on with our status quo.

As you continue to accumulate knowledge about yourself and the world and you think about where you are and where you want to go, it's my hope that you find what works for you. Honor your own process and whatever time that may take.

Often, for us worriers, when we look at a problem, we think of 101 ways to fail. However, reframing a question by starting with *"How might I..."* lifts you from anxiety to wonder and to hope. *"How might I..."* on its own has the power to transform our thoughts and bring us to more open-ended thinking. It's a phrase I learned from the founders of the d. school at Stanford University. Even Amber Rae, in her book *Choose Wonder over Worry*, shares this sentiment.[87]

But the learning process isn't always skill-based or assessed by content acquisition. Sometimes, the best learning we can give ourselves is understanding that we need help. That *we're* the one in need. That we can't do it alone.

So, how might we change our questions to better reflect our desired outcome? How might our questions lead us closer to what's really on our hearts?

Start by setting intentions. Decide how we want this year, this day, this moment to go. Determine what our non-negotiables are for how we want to show up in the classroom. Examine the values we and our school hold. It's OK if you don't have those answers right now. That's where tuning into the voice that nurtures you can help.

It may sound scary, but it's actually quite simple. The answers are already in you. To uncover what's there, let's ask the questions: *Who? What? Why?*

Your *Who* is who you are doing this for. And so, maybe it might make sense to see *What* you're doing first. What change are you looking to make? What is the thing that's frustrating you so much you can't take another second of it? What tugs at your heart when you're trying to fall asleep? What do you want to see differently? Do you want to respond to children differently? Do you want to give yourself grace for your mistakes? What is the thing that is important to you *right now?* What do you want?

When I decided to stop drinking, my "What" was very clear: abstain from alcohol. I didn't want it anymore. I didn't want to want it anymore. Which led me to my "Why." *I knew what would happen if I didn't change. I didn't know what could happen if I did.* For me, my drinking life wasn't necessarily bad, but it wasn't serving me any longer. I knew that if I continued with drinking, I was certain my life would look like "X." And I kinda, sorta wanted it to look like "Y." Or some arrangement I had never dreamed of! And that was my *Why.* I was so curious, so damn curious, about "Y." I wanted to go somewhere new.

When days got hard, or I'd watch a TV show and feel FOMO or triggered to have a drink, I'd remind myself of my *Why.* It wasn't always easy, but for me, I was surprised by how much easier it was than I had expected it to be. Of course, there are a lot of factors behind that, but I felt my Why was always clear and in focus to help guide me on the days I wanted to look elsewhere. And because I had that Why, and I knew what changes I wanted to make, I had a clear foundation. My safety harness was buckled.

Because of the solid foundation my clear Why and What gave me, I also knew Who I was doing this for. It wasn't my husband. It wasn't my kids. It was for me. Naturally, they were sideline beneficiaries of this decision, as were the students in my class, but all the changes I wanted to see were for me to build myself up in a new way.

It so happened that my decision to stop drinking occurred during the same school year I led with W.W.M.R.D—*What Would Mr. Rogers Do?* Changes in my professional life helped my personal life and vice versa. I was inspired by Mr. Rogers because of the way he treated children with gentle respect, love, and belonging. My Why for that decision really had to do with the children. And I say that because, again, when it got tough, I needed to remember who I was doing this for just like with my sobriety.

Now that you've started thinking about your Who, What, and Why, perhaps you're wondering When to start.

There may never be a "right" time to make a change, but I trust the more you get acquainted with the desires of your heart, you will also learn to trust your timing. It knocks, knocks, and knocks until you're ready to open the door.

Still, because this work is about our lives in and out of the classroom, it feels especially impactful to set your intentions before ever crossing the threshold of the new school year. It can put your whole year in focus.

I've found it particularly helpful to start during the summer and, if I'm lucky enough, before the end of the prior school year. If I knew I was going to be in the same position and classroom for the upcoming school year, I made sure to intentionally clean and organize before my summer break. I'm not going to lie; I was usually one of the last teachers still around the building at closing time. I can only hope that one year the End-of-Year-Gods will grace me with the quickness and efficiency displayed by some of my former colleagues. Until then, I will never understand how they clean up their room so quickly! (Alas, we all have different strengths and weaknesses.)

Knowing that I was going to give myself time to organize, I methodically put away materials so that they'd be ready for the start of the year. But the real work started once the classroom was closed up. In early August, when the school dreams started (you know those ones), and I couldn't deny the Back-to-School displays any longer, I got my first flash of inspiration. First, worry, panic, fear, and dread. But, not so far after, inspiration! I call this my "teacher nesting," akin to when mothers want to prepare the nursery for the arrival of the baby. I was full of the motivation and drive to prepare my classroom. *Bins, bins, all the bins!*

But something I realized was that work had less to do with physical setup and more about preparing my mind. Before school even started, I made decisions about how I wanted my year to go. Again, it starts with getting really clear on what's important to you. In other words, it's about making yourself a priority.

Having an intention for your year, or even broken up into smaller increments, can help you regain focus on your priorities. Sweets, I hope you're learning by now this includes you, too. You deserve your own love.

So, what is going to give you the year you want?

You can look at your goals strictly for the classroom, or you can also set intentions for your year that encompass your whole self, that is, how you envision your life as a teacher to be—your life that includes teaching but is not all about teaching. Mothers and parents can relate to this a lot. When you are in the thick of parenting, especially little children, it's very easy to lose sight of who you are. Or what you did in the days before this became your role. And when you're in the trenches, the boiler rooms, the sticky floor of your kitchen, you can easily forget how to be new again.

This is one way to get back on the path of you.

Still, I understand how difficult it can be for us to measure our progress. We forget how far we have come. We lose sight of where we want to go. One thing that has really helped me on both of these accounts is reviewing my teaching portfolio. Not sure how this might help? Let's dust off that ol' thing and have a look.

After having a visible breakdown in the classroom in March of 2018, I decided—that very night, actually—to begin looking for new work. I could not take the demands of full-time teaching while also trying to raise my twins, who were not even one year old.

And I was tired. I was tired of hearing myself say that I wanted a change professionally and doing nothing about it. You know that quote, the one that goes, if you get jealous watching somebody do something you love, then you know that's what you need to do? That summed up how I felt about any teacher doing specific literacy work. I was tired of being the classroom teacher. I was tired of holding all of the parts together. I couldn't take one more student throwing my classroom materials into the hallway. And I certainly couldn't take the guilt and shame I felt for being a crappy teacher.

I did what I believe to be one of the most important things an educator can do: revise my résumé. At this point, I had already worked in three separate schools. So, this was not the first time I had to reconsider my needs and wants. From doing it before, I learned how valuable it was to me.

Reviewing my résumé, specifically my cover letter, didn't necessarily mean I would work elsewhere. Still, it helped me redefine what I had learned since my last placement. It allowed me to see if my philosophy was evolving and if anything new interested me.

With the confidence and self-assurance of my prior experiences, I felt the privilege of really honing in on what positions interested me and saying no to what did not fit me at this time. For weeks after the meltdown, I continued to browse online job boards and tweak my portfolio, making it more precise and presentable.

Finally, I saw a dream listing: "Kindergarten Reading Support." It was everything I was looking for. But there were two problems. It was part-time and at a private school.

Part-time work meant that I'd be bringing in a significant change to my salary. And private? Ugh! I prided myself on being a public school teacher! I had always attended public schools. I had only ever worked at public schools. I loved everything they stood for. In fact, my first three years subbing and teaching, I worked in the district where I had been a student. It was both a joy and an honor to be a part of the community in this new way.

Looking at it now, I see how much my home district felt like family to me. Private schools were foreign to me. Would I fit in? Would I belong there?

I decided to apply anyway.

I was overjoyed when I got a call back for an interview. I spent the next two weeks diligently discussing our finances with my husband and trying to see if there was still a path forward for me at my current school. When I was offered the Kindergarten Reading Support position, I knew I had to say yes.

Even if you do not plan to leave your current position, reviewing your résumé shows you what you value. It allows you to pull back the curtain slightly to see what else is possible. It often brings pride and gratitude for what you've accomplished. In best-case scenarios, it shows you if you want to quit. But not always in the way you imagined. Sometimes, quitting can be a quiet strength.

For a few weeks in 2023, I heard and saw the term "quiet quitting" pop up across newsfeeds. Like the very non-trendsetter I am, I dismissed it. I imagined it had to do with quitting your job without notice; frankly, I didn't care enough to look into it further. Then, at a WalMart checkout, a young twenty-something gazed at me from the front cover of a magazine. The words in print came into view: "In Defence of Gen Z."[88] I was ready to dismiss it again, being very over our obsessions with differentiating millennials and boomers, and so on. But then, the bold statement by Stephanie Bai captivated me. She said, "My generation values work-life balance over hustle culture. You call it lazy. We call it smart". I bought the issue on the spot.

This. This is what I've been searching for.

That evening, I did what any sane, responsible adult does these days and googled, "quiet quitting." I was amazed to realize I was wrong about my assumptions. It wasn't some "dumb millennial term" that felt trendy and viral, nor was it due to the person's lack of responsibility. It was everything I, too, was—*AM*—searching for. It was a way to reprioritize your relationship to your work.

Over the past few years, as I wrestled with the *do I stay or do I go* question, my decision to return to the classroom had everything to do with how teaching aligned with my mental and physical health. It's also why I had to show up here. Teachers are tired and in need of love. They need someone who understands them, pulling them along. Those struggling the most need to know they're not alone.

If I'm being totally honest, I'm still afraid to return to the classroom. I'm afraid I won't have what it takes anymore. I'm afraid my softened, wants-to-live-an-easier-life kinda way won't be able to stand up to the challenge of full-time teaching. I'm afraid that as much as I've learned about myself these past few years, particularly in how to own who I am, it will all crumble when I'm face-to-face with my first battle. When that first look of disappointment washes over a parent's face, when that child won't sit still, when it feels like all I do is work.

I'm afraid I won't have time for my family. I'm afraid this tender and true space I've created for sharing my writing and my heart will fade. I'm so afraid of what I may lose.

And still, by saying these fears aloud and asking myself what's really going on, I'm reminded of the power I do have. I'm reminded I've been here before. When we moved from Pennsylvania to California, as scared as I was to make that big change, I had to remind myself then: *Life cannot be mapped. There could always be change.*

At that moment, I was more excited for what could go right than what could go wrong.

And right now, I'm doing that again.

Things will grow if we take the time to nurture them.

I still haven't learned it all. I'm still afraid of going in before I can swim. Yet, by understanding that I already have so much power in me, I'm reminded that I can go to new places simply by reframing my questions and fears. When I sink into the truth of who I am, I remember that today is a new day and that I am in control of myself, and I can breathe. I can feel my way forward. I can find a way. My way may not be your way, but that is OK. Your way may not be mine, and that is fine. We still get to do this together. And, together, we can do anything.

Consider This:

- Fill in the sentence, *"I feel best when ...."*
- Review your most recent résumé and cover letter. What has changed for you since your last placement? What feels most important to you now?

14

Come Full Circle

> *Every thing that's ever been
> has led me to this moment.*

You made it. We made it. We're here: the last chapter. But I know your story will go beyond these pages. It must. You're not done yet. There's so much good coming your way.

Waters, roads, bridges, floods, tsunamis, storms—I've used so many metaphors throughout these pages. But they all have something in common.

Each time I've traversed a new landscape, I scraped my knees. Sometimes, I wondered if I'd ever make it to my destination. The ground below me would drop. With it went my hopes, dreams, and the version of me I was then. Yet, each time I've fallen, eventually, I've gotten back up. One day, I penned this poem to remind myself about this impermanence:

Rise, Fall
We love to rise.
We hate to fall.
Yet, in order to breathe,
In order to live,
We need both.

But would I have known that if I was never taught thoughts are not facts? Would I be able to honor the *both* if I didn't read somewhere that two truths can coexist? Where would I be if I never learned to sharpen my tools?

Would I have really, truly felt this in my soul if I never broke into a million pieces?

I recently read that we don't need to be grateful for our pain or believe it happened for "a reason" to still make something of it. Author, Theology Professor, and cancer survivor Kate Bowler says we don't need to think the pain was "worth it," and yet, from that pain, we can, and often do, gain a new perspective. We become more deeply human. We know what it's like to become more deeply human.

While out for a walk one brisk February morning when the sun was fighting with the temperature outside, I ungloved my dry, cracked hands to snap a photo of a planter box at the corner of an intersection. Painted as a warning to drivers, it read: "CAUTION, Humans Ahead!"

My immediate thought was, *"I need to put this as a sign on my classroom door!"* Because ain't that the truth? In its most basic and complete form, a classroom is full of people. People err. People have feelings. People need so much. How are we not supposed to exercise caution when our work as educators is to teach people and love them well? How can we do that if we don't see them as a person first? If we don't see ourselves as a human worth loving?

I often wondered if I should include so much of my personal story in a book that's for you. But I've learned that if I can't see myself for the whole individual I am, I cannot see my students as themselves. I can't fully grasp who they are, to whom they're connected, and what constitutes their life outside school walls. Nor could I do that for you.

In honoring me, I create room to honor you, too.

I honor my full self so that I may honor yours.

I love my full self so I may love yours.

I meet my needs so I may help you meet yours.

Where it ends is where it starts. And we just need to start.

Yet, perhaps, it's a restart we're really looking for.

By now, in 2024, we know that mental health discussions must be on the table. And, if they're not, it's time to redecorate. Yet, when we boil it down even further, it's not just "mental health" that's in question; it's how we look at student achievement. It's how we look at *our* achievements.

When we right-size our expectations, when we see our students are able to do more even while we do less, we give ourselves space and ease.

Our means need to matter.

Not too long ago, I was fervently on the side of more, more, more. And now all I want to scream is, "Less, less, less."

Feel better, do less.

And, our "less" wouldn't even be catastrophic. It would be... *sustainable.* More humanity, less pressure. More support, fewer loose ends. More financial backing, less under-compensation. More dignity, less mockery. Teachers shouldn't have to shout from the rooftops for people to hear what we want—what we really, really want—is the financial and emotional security to make the career we chose and love sustainable.

Teachers don't want to leave. But for so many, their hands are tied. They simply cannot carry on under these conditions. *Do you stay or do you go?*

Teacher, I think you're reading this because you want to stay. You made it this far because you're not hopeless. You're actually hope-filled, in the tired wanting-things-to-be-different kind of way. I believe you're doing whatever you can to make this *work* work for you. That is what *I'm* doing, after all. I didn't write this book for those who have, respectfully, decided they are out of the game. I wrote it for those who are staying. For those who might have left but realize they want back in. For those who need a way to make this *work* contribute to their life. Because you deserve so, so much teacher and you deserve a career that sustains and fills you. This work should not empty your bucket. And unfortunately, I know that it has.

But there is a way for us to fill it again.

In our pursuit of the unattainable best, we lost sight of how to treat ourselves with care. In the face of disaster and tragedy, we forgot to care for our bodies. And, maybe, perhaps, we were never taught. Now you know it can be learned.

Whether in school or out, I can't operate with the weight of the world on my back anymore. And I know you don't want to either. When I take care of my mental health by re-learning how to treat myself and manage my expectations (and limitations), I give myself the ultimate power: freedom. I am free to do the work I love so dearly because I'm not at risk of imploding. I'm not a threat to myself by way of a demeaning inner critic. This work is too important for us to be hurt by our own words.

I hope that moving forward, you see that there's no perfect way, no one right way. And when the way you chose no longer feels right, you stop and take notice. You find out why that is, but you don't dwell. You accept and trust that it's not good for you anymore, and you move on. You find the next thing that feels right. This doesn't cause you to look back on your past choices with shame and stall. It allows you to have grace for what you didn't know then.

If you had asked yourself if it felt right, you probably would have said yes. That's how it works. But now you see things differently, and that's OK. Maybe you don't know what the next right thing is yet. That's OK, too. Because you will, even if that takes a little time.

Sometimes, it's easier and simpler than you think. You learn to trust and listen to your body because your body knows. Even when you're stuck, I believe deep down you know the way to your healing. But it does require quiet and listening.

I hope that when it feels like it's taking more time than you'd like, you *do* have the patience to wait it out. You see, you already possess this strength, as frustrating as it can be sometimes. *Not happening right now* is not the same as *not happening ever*. It's all part of the timeline of you. In the waiting period, the patience period, I hope that you also do not dwell. Because *here* is not forever. *Impermanence.*

Mostly, I hope you build self-compassion for yourself. The greatest hug you've ever been given. Squeezing life into you instead of out. I hope your inner voice becomes the voice of love. After all, it knows you best. And it's been waiting for you to tell it to proceed. It craves compassion. It's just a little stuck somewhere between a hurt child and pissed-off teenager. But the voice of You knows love. Aren't you ready for a change?

I do not wish to look back on my experiences with shame anymore. I want to have more compassion for what I accomplished and grace for what fell short. I want to see that *being unable to do it all* didn't make me a lousy teacher; it made me an average human. A normal human who faced a landslide of stress. When I do this, I remind myself of my humanity and know I can keep going. I can carry on when it gets tricky. I don't have to be perfect anymore.

Yet, it's impossible to know it all your first year; that would make you perfect, and that doesn't exist (sorry, younger Christina). I learned sixteen years after obtaining my degree that there's no perfect teacher, just as there's no perfect parent. You learn. You learn some more. And you keep just doing your best. The rest can fall away.

But what I'm also seeing is how I've come full circle.

For sixteen years, the cover of my teaching portfolio has been a clipart design with the slogan: "Committed to Success." For so long, "Committed to Success" meant that I was going to do whatever it took to not let anyone down. I was going to be the best at all costs.

I sure paid for it.

The phrase carried me for a distance. Until it didn't. Until I couldn't go anymore. Until my legs were so battered from falling, and my hands were heavy with grief.

As I began to think of this book, that phrase came back to me, and that cover came back with questions. *What* am I committed to now? *Who* am I committed to now? And what does *success* even look like?!

In trying to be the best, we completely lose sight of ourselves. We forget that, or perhaps never learned, that we can err. We forget, or maybe never knew, we cannot control everything. We forget, or perhaps never learned, that our pursuits, commitments, and success are cloaked in perfectionism and disguised as friendly behaviors but are harborers of hate if not overseen. We don't realize that we've set ourselves up for failure in committing to success. Because when we equate success with perfection, there is never a winner. The bar is continually raised higher.

At time of this press, that Microsoft Word clipart design still rests on my portfolio, but a new message has landed on my heart: *We are enough*. It doesn't take away our commitments, it reframes them.

We can be committed to the success of our hearts and our souls.

We can be committed to the unveiling of our humanity.

We can be committed to the success of our kindness, our cares, and our contributions.

You get to define what "success" means to you. Teachers, administrators, board members, politicians, your spouse, your child, that Instagram influencer will all try to tell you what success means to them. They'll disguise it as what success should look like for you. But only you get to measure. Because you get to pour. And Dear Teacher, I hope you pour into you.

We don't need a marker telling us if we got the job done. The job will never be done. But we can live now with present and full hearts, using compassion and the spirit of tenacity to see another day. To teach another lesson. To open another door. I believe this with every ounce of my being. And I am committed to helping you see it, too.

These are the things I wish I could have told younger me:

You don't have to have it all figured out.

You can make mistakes.

You can't do this work perfectly.

At some point, some children will be beyond your capacity to help.

(It's OK to ask for help.)

Children are not the problem. The parents are not the problem. The way we've been living with massive expectations and unexamined mental wellness is the problem. The system of no-support and improper funding is the problem. Every school I worked at was beautiful. This is not a discussion or disparagement of any particular building, teacher, child, or administration but of education as a whole. Of our Teacherhood, our livelihood as teachers.

That's what the heart of this work is. It all returns to the same vein: loving yourself and owning who you are. That's what this work has always been about. It's been about finding, honoring, and encompassing all the parts of you. The messy parts, the vices, the joy, and the justice. The essence of you.

It is my hope that we enter into a new phase of education where educators and teachers can feel free to express who they are. That fear of showing ourselves is replaced with warmth and empathy and compassion.

Could we—maybe —just make some room for ourselves? Could we stop hiding?

Can we come to love who we are and not feel like parts of us need to be shelved just because we are educators?

Can we dispel the "perfect mom myth," which is also the perfect teacher myth, and find a way to allow teachers to show their full humanity, anger, and all?

Could we, as a nation and a world, do this?

Just imagine a place where people are not afraid to be who they are. Imagine the freedom that comes along with the space to exist. Imagine what that would do for our children to see that we do not need to be shame-filled and worry-centered.

And I share this because, as teachers, we are expected to do right by both children and adults. We're not quite stating this, but the message heard is: be perfect or else.

This idea that I couldn't "mess up" made it incredibly hard to reach out when I was struggling. I didn't want to shatter my image of perfection. I didn't want to be seen as incapable or immoral. I didn't want others to see that sometimes I get angry at kids. I didn't want them to know that I didn't know how to best proceed in a situation. I didn't want them to see that my home life could be messy, too.

So, how might we begin to make space for our very human making-of-mistakes? It starts right here. It starts with radically recognizing that you will make mistakes AND THIS IS OK. It does not devalue you, dewarrant you, or decapitate you. Though if you do lose your head for a moment, you can put it back on. You can tighten the screws and create more internal stability.

I came to realize I could make mistakes by hearing this message over and over and over again from people whom I trusted. People whom I knew cared for me AND have been in my shoes before. I needed that reassurance that "they really knew" what it was like.

But before I had another person to lean on, I had to be my own advocate, my own cheerleader. Now you know how to do that for yourself, too. Recall that we started our time together with a note from me to you. We will end this same way. When stressful times and worry consume me, I like to write a note for my future self. Typically, five years into the future. I want to write from the perspective that I achieved the things in my heart while also recognizing there were bumps. The road wasn't entirely smooth, and yet I made it across. There's one such letter for you at the end of this book. Please read it and take it upon yourself to rewrite your story. I've included directions and tips to get you started.

And as time passes, and you're in need of a path to take, recall the ones offered to you in this work.

Pause

Ask what's really going on

Think about what you need, and

Hold on to your humanity.

Let these words be a buoy when you're caught off-guard. A light post when you can't find your way. Remember that you will cycle. This is the nature of life and impermanence. Thankfully, I've paved a way for you to receive the support you need. You don't have to ignore what's happening. You can:

Keep Calm **AND**

Cry a Little or A lot

Name Your Feelings

Name Your Grief

Give Yourself Grace and Self-Compassion

Remind Yourself You're Not Alone

And That You Can Do This, so

Dust Off the Cheeto Powder

Do the Next Thing

And then, and only then,

CARRY ON.

It's a path you can take over and over again. Hop, skip, or jump as you need. Walk or run. Take in the views when you're at the beach and put on flashers through the fog. The path doesn't need to be linear, either. You can turn it into a round-about. You are the traffic controller and the driver.

That is the beauty of where I sit. I've been in, and I've been out. I've seen education from the perspective of a student, a teacher, a parent, and an executive board president. I've seen it up close and personal and from the sidelines. I've tried to run as far away as possible from it. And it caught back up with me. The conversation is not over.

Because in this still sort of place of unknowing, I know this: you deserve to be seen. You deserve to be celebrated. You deserve to be treated like the human being you are. Teaching may be your life, but you are still a person first.

Until we can see that, honor that, and come face-to-face with this truth, things will not change. They will stay the same. It will only get harder.

But, thankfully, I believe there's another way.

I believe we're in a unique position as both people who continually strive for better and people who are nurturing and accepting our limitations to find that sweet spot of soul justice. We can take back the reins and pull ourselves toward what we want. What our souls crave: love, belonging, connection, and purpose.

We can create the life we want by teaching what's on our hearts. From our heart. With our hearts. We do this by seeking our humanity first and honoring the spirit within us.

This light can also guide you when nothing goes right. Because, unfortunately, dear teacher, we're in the world of everything going wrong all of the time. And it's not just in the classroom because everything outside comes in. That's the nature of working with people.

We change education, not by a single lesson or switching materials, but by the philosophy of how we treat people. If we cannot see the people—the adults and the children—we work with as people, we cannot help them. Nor can we do that for ourselves. Systems do not get better if we do not take care of those in the system. We must hold the practice of compassion in our hands and extend it to others. It's simple but true. We cannot pour from an empty cup. I've tried to avoid the reality of this statement too many times to count. I've tried to imagine I am somehow immune from the challenges of serving my children when I am barely holding it together. I believed the illusion that I could do it all because I was in survival mode. Admitting that I couldn't, would have broken me. But that's where the deception lies. I was already broken. I was cracked. I could hold no more. I just didn't want to admit it.

You do what works until what you did doesn't work anymore.

You do what works until what you did doesn't work anymore.

You do what works until what you did doesn't work anymore.

What we were doing no longer works. And it's OK to say that. It's OK to feel that. It's even OK to be disappointed and frustrated that you need to pivot one more time.

For so long, I thought if I held on to my oars tightly enough, I would make it through anything. But when the waters became tough and then rougher, I finally had to sink into the words my husband had been telling me all along: "Things will always be tough. This is life," he said. But I didn't want to see it that way. I wanted to moan and bemoan these circumstances. I wanted to moan and kick away this new thing inching its way toward my life. I was so tired of one more thing getting in my way. "This is life," he said. I wanted to bat those words so far out of the park. I wanted to punt them into another field. I didn't want them anywhere near me. And yet, after months and months of turmoil and tension, much of which was out of my control, I began to hear the faintest whisper of truth in his message. A loving, patient therapist also helped. For as much as I did learn in 36 years of being alive, I hadn't learned to accept how hard life can be.

But now I live in a new land.

Recognizing my own humanity was a bridge I'd been waiting my whole life to cross. It took me somewhere new. Over time, it allowed me to venture to foreign places like *Worth*. I learned I didn't have to do anything to earn my worth. I was inherently worthy.

This was everything.

It was as revolutionary as learning about mindfulness. Yet, as life-changing as the revelations about mindfulness were, they occurred in 2014, over a decade ago—before California, before postpartum, before Canada, and before the pandemic.

I include this because we expect results quickly. We expect to learn things once and not have to learn them again. We expect things to stick. But when things get sticky, we want to run the other way. We want to wash our hands clean. We want to remove any inkling of failure.

And as I've learned, that is not the sea we swim in. Those are not the waters we wade. Life will take us great distances. Far and wide. It will lift us to mounting heights and watch as we cascade down under the surface. It will flow rapidly and come to a slow trickle. We are the water and the stream. The doer and the doing. And the sooner we realize we aren't entitled to anything, that life isn't simply going to be handed to us without caution, the faster we become free.

We become free to bask in the glory of who we are. We become free to settle our score. We become free to throw it all away. We are new once again.

Self-compassion is the balm I never knew I needed. It saved my life. I am not sure where I'd be if I didn't learn it. If I had not gone to that therapy appointment, at the precise time, everything in my life would have fallen apart. If I didn't start writing down my truths, my hard. If I never started to talk to myself like a friend in my "Self-Compassion and Grace Journal," if I hadn't listened to Celion Dion's, *O Holy Night,* 42 times in a row on Christmas Eve night, 2019. Each listen, the refrain of "worth" becoming more resounding and clear. If I hadn't let myself be angry and sad during the whole of 2020, and again in 2021, and again in 2022. If I didn't text my friend when I thought dying would be easier than living. And if I never decided that, more than anything, I knew you needed to hear this message, too.

You are more than anything you'll ever know. More than anything, you'll ever think or do, or say, or become, or teach. Because you are You. There is no taking that away.

You will have failure beyond measure. You'll worry if you've made the wrong choice. If your tone of voice or lack of empathy last week will scar your children, your students... *Hey, you still with me? It won't.*

> *Breathe into the pinhole.*
> *And go to the other side.*
> *Receive all that you have to offer.*
> *You are worth it.*

You are the master of your classroom, the leader in pursuit. You get to do it all and nothing, too. You get to make the decisions. And most importantly, you get to make the decisions for you. The ones that set you apart from who you were yesterday, last year, a week ago. You are allowed to want to fight this. To resist that this is something you may need to do for yourself. Friend, this is OK, too. It's not a race. It's OK if it takes time.

Because you're in it for the long haul. Your classroom, your teaching, means the world to you. So let it. But don't forget yourself in the process.

Decide what's important for you. And let it be OK if it changes. It's OK if it changes. You are dynamic. Not static. You are always in motion. Let it be towards a place you want to call home.

Your rest is up to you.

Consider This:

- What does success look like for you today? How might you allow yourself to adjust this criterion as you learn and grow?
- You will always be who this work is for. What will you carry with you moving forward?

Epilogue

A Letter to Future You

H ello, Love,
     I can't believe it's been five years since you read this book. Seriously! Where does the time go? I know how skeptical you felt when you began to read this. Those years were hard. Really hard. On top of just coming out of the pandemic, you were still dealing with life! So you wondered, would this book feel like one more thing? Would you get something out of it? Friend, I am so glad you carried on. Because what a blessing it's been to see you from afar.

You went from a person who was always down on yourself to someone who recognizes when they're being too harsh. You notice when your thoughts dwell on small details, and you've learned to breathe and let go. I am so proud of you. And I mean that most sincerely. You didn't grow up with these lessons. These are things you had to learn yourself. And you did! And I know at times it felt like self-improvement and self-healing were a never-ending game, but you are so much further than you think. You're doing so much better than you believe. I know you can't always see it, but I do. And your friends and colleagues do, too.

I know some days it feels like someone threw soap on the floor, and you've slipped back into old habits. Your room's a mess, and the kids won't listen. It feels like you've got nowhere to stand—and so much information is coming your way! Decision paralysis smacks you in the face. *Breathe.* It's going to be OK. You are stronger than you were before. You've learned tenacity. You've witnessed your resilience.

I get it. Those days that don't go as planned are hard. The days that come out of nowhere and steal our breath away—those days, for better or worse, are unavoidable. We can try as we might to not let them touch us, but then we're in a race we'll never win. As writer and speaker Layla F. Saad says, "Expect the expected." Life won't always come at us the way we wish. We will have times of struggle alongside times of joy. But when we know this, when we better understand that we aren't owed a "perfect life," we begin to let go. I'm so proud of you for finding ways to release the need to have it all together. From gripping to the illusion of control to feeling like you needed to be responsible for everything and everyone. You've recognized what's most important to you and have found little ways to release the rest. By doing this, you've given yourself a green light to go wild.

So go wild!

And...

It's OK to slow down. It's OK to fall. The good times won't always last. But, dear, remember this: *Impermanence.* At least you'll know when to get back up.

I am so proud of you because when you started this book, you weren't sure where you were. You weren't sure where you were going. You just sought a change. I know you can't fully believe you are where you are now! But you did that! You did the thing. You found a way to let the smallest ray of grace touch your face. You made room for patience to fill your pockets on the slow days of waiting. You've found someone you can confide in.

Not every day went as you had hoped. We can't be perfect. But you're learning, this is OK. (I know, I know, *why hasn't this one stuck yet?!*) Take it from me: this is the long game. We can learn it and relearn it as many times as necessary. You are always becoming. And when you've reached your limit—because you will, and because you have—it's OK to stop. To say, "Enough is enough." Because, friend, you are *always enough*. And what you do doesn't define your worth. Keep going. I love you.

With all the love that remains,

In gratitude and pleasure,

XO, Christina

Reach out if you need me // thecouragetoday@gmail.com

Acknowledgments

First, I'd like to thank Brian Dixon and the team at hope*books Publishing for having the vision to bring a group of us together to write the books on our hearts. I'm forever grateful that you saw the need for these words to be in the hands of teachers, too. Your tireless, behind-the-scenes work carried this book from beginning to end. Thank you, thank you, thank you.

To my early editors, Sarah and Molly, your extra enthusiasm and cheerleading made me believe I could do this. And that I had the magic to pull it off! You're awesome.

To Tj Ray, you held this book in its infancy and gave it room to grow. I'm forever grateful for your guidance, patience, and support. Thank you for showing me I didn't have to use so many f-bombs to have impact. Gloria Day and Rachel Hankinson, thank you for helping me bring this work home.

To Krissy Nelson and the entire cohort of authors, especially my beloved November crew, I'm so grateful our paths crossed. You've taught me so much. May we keep leading each other forward.

To the cited authors, writers, and creatives who came before me. Thank you for sharing your brave and insightful words. They made this book have an even greater depth.

An additional thank you to Taylor S. Schumann for opening the virtual doors to your *Writing in the Cracks* cohort. You made me feel like my words belonged. I'm so indebted to your kindness and vision for creating that very needed writing group.

To my friends and family, from long-form emails to family newsletters, thank you for being my first audience and supporting my visions! I love you.

To my friends and companions on IG and social media, thank you for making the world a little brighter and more connected. You'll always be more than your content.

For all the subscribers to my newsletter and readers of *The Good Teacher Series*, I'm so honored I get to share my heart with you each week. Thank you for letting me be in your life.

To my loves, my LYLAS, you own my heart. Kiley, Evelynn, Natalie, Shannon, and Ricque, I know you're always there for me. To those I met on my way home, Ana, Lisa, Kelley, Kristin, Emma, Marina, Olga, and Alexandra, you show me unconditional love every time we connect. <3

I'm also so thankful for the community of friends we've made in Vancouver after a very lonely period. I'm so glad our kiddos are growing up together. And that we are witnesses to each other's lives.

When it comes to teachers—YOU—reading this, you've always been who this work is for. May you feel seen and heard in these pages. You will always, always be enough.

To my colleagues and teacher friends from Erie and Oakland. Where do I even begin? I'd put you on my teacher all-star roster any day.

Extra thanks to Darlene Dovichow for providing your story to this work. The world needs more of you.

I'm thankful (again) for you, Dov and Carrie, Kylene, Dana G., Lori, Karin, and Ryan, for taking me under your wing. Your mentorship and support made me feel special, loved, and prepared. Once a Mariner, always a Mariner. And to Janie, Lisa, and Tammy, thanks for letting me be the new girl. To past administrators: Dana S., Anthony, Erin (although we never got to really meet), Tiama, David, and Jill—thank you for seeing something in me.

To Freedom, to David, to Kristi, Colleen, Laurel, Jennifer, and Malorie, thank you for your patience. I know I wasn't always the easiest to work with, and I thank you for all that you taught me.

To the precious schools where I worked, full of the families and children who make this world more beautiful, you remind me why we do this work. Thank you for being you.

To my father-in-law, John, who called me while I was on the Skytrain and was the first person to ask where you could purchase this book. I'll never forget that moment. It made me realize this dream was coming true. For anyone who has asked about the book—near and far—it means more than you know.

To my therapist Erin, who's proof that changing one life can change many, there would be no book without you. And, possibly, no me. You've shown me what a steady, loving witness can do to a person. There will never be enough thank yous.

To my parents, Sue and Tom, who've been my number one supporters from the start. Thank you for always believing in me and giving me the runway to dream. No one can replace you. I love you so much.

To my daughters, Roa and Gwenevere, thank you for sharing your mama with her writing. Your endless questions of, "Is your book done yet?" and "Are you writing again?" held me accountable. But mostly, I held pride and love in being witnessed by you, especially when you gifted me pens and notebooks. Even with all the grief and upset life brings, may you know how much I love you. I'll always love you. You remind me every day that joy is at my fingertips.

Lastly, to my husband, partner, and friend of over 20 years, John—there's a whole book with our story in it. (Maybe I won't write that one just yet.) I'm so glad to be doing life with you. Thank you for choosing, over and over again, to make life with me, even when I forget to *Silencio Bruno*. This book would not have been possible without your endless support and sacrifice and, above all else, your unconditional love. More than anyone, you're my safe person. My shore. My harbor. As then, as it is now, *I need you so much closer.* Thank you a million times over.

And, to all the previous versions of me: I'm so proud of you.
Thank you for not giving up.
You got us here.

Bibliography

Chapter One

1. Impermanence. *Oxford English Dictionary*, 2nd ed., vol. 5, Oxford University Press, 1989.

2. Hawthorne, Britt. "Blog." Britt Hawthorne, 2024, www.britthawthorne.com/blog/. Accessed 22 September 2024.

3. Bone, Jamina. *"You Are Still a Good Mom."* Jamina Bone, 2024, jaminabone.com/series/still-a-good-mom. This series highlights a challenge to social expectations around motherhood emphasizing that even if a mother feels overwhelmed, imperfect, or struggles with guilt, these feelings do not take away from her worth as a parent.

Additional Reading:

Brown, Brené. *Dare to Lead: Brave Work. Tough Conversations. Whole Hearts.* Random House, 2018.

Chapter Two

1. Siegel, Daniel J., and Tina Payne Bryson. *The Whole Brain Child: 12 Revolutionary Strategies to Nurture Your Child's Developing Mind.* Delacorte Press, 2011.

2. Gallup, Inc. "Workers with Highest Burnout Rate." *Gallup*, 26 May 2022, www.gallup.com/poll/393500/workers-highest-burnout-rate.aspx.

3. Peck, Devlin. "Teacher Burnout Statistics." *Devlin Peck*, www.devlinpeck.com/content/teacher-burnout-statistics#:~:text=6.,(The%20Wall%20Street%20Journal). Accessed 18 August. 2024.

4. National Education Association. *NEA Active Minds Presentation.* 14 June 2024, www.nea.org/sites/default/files/2024-06/nea-active-minds-presentation-final-6-14-24.pdf. Accessed 3 August 2024.

5. Peck, Devlin. "Teacher Burnout Statistics." *Devlin Peck*, www.devlinpeck.com/content/teacher-burnout-statistics#:~:text=6.,(The%20Wall%20Street%20Journal). Accessed 18 August 2024.

6. Dion, Lisa. *Printable - Synergetic Play Therapy Institute.* Synergetic Play Therapy Institute, 2021, www.synergeticplaytherapy.com/wp-content/uploads/2021/07/NS-Handout_2021.pdf. Accessed 18 August 2024.

7. Dion, Lisa. Ibid.

8. Center on the Developing Child. *Key Concepts: Toxic Stress.* Harvard University, https://developingchild.harvard.edu/science/key-concepts/toxic-stress/. Accessed 3 September 2024.

9. van der Kolk, Bessel A. "The Body Keeps the Score: Brain, Mind, and Body in the Healing of Trauma." Penguin Books, 2014.
Author Note: *As I learn more about my own children, particularly as it pertains to nervous system regulation, I recognize that I was taught this. My early psychology courses and teacher prep did teach us about the body's survival system. That begs me to ask: why have we forgotten about this?*

10. Freeman, Emily P. *The Next Right Thing: A Simple, Soulful Practice for Making Life Decisions.* WaterBrook, 2019.

Chapter Three

1. Standing, E.M. *Maria Montessori: Her Life and Work*. 2nd ed., Plume, 1998.

2. Harper, Amber. *Burned-In Teacher*. www.burnedinteacher. com.

Chapter Four

1. Collins, Kathy. *Growing Readers: Lessons from a Teacher's Heart*. Stenhouse Publishers, 2009.

2. Calkins, Lucy. *Units of Study for Teaching Writing*. Heinemann, 2003.

3. *Author's Note: In 2022, Lucy Calkins came under fire for her long standing approach to literacy development. Many critics argued that the "workshop" style of teaching reading and writing, employed by Calkins and her colleagues, was not effective, particularly for marginalized communities. It's been heavily criticized for not explicitly teaching phonics or the skills of reading. As a longtime proponent of Calkins, and the whole of the TCRWP, I was shocked and at a loss of how to proceed. I'm aware of the arguments *and* I've seen the success of these approaches in combination with other foundational literacy components. Has your school dealt with this? Where do you stand?

4. RuPaul. "Inner Saboteur." *W Magazine*, www.wmagazine. com/story/rupaul-inspiring-quotes-rupauls-drag-race. Accessed 8 September. 2024.

5. Author's Note: Actually, I've learned writing a book *is* hard work. Don't let anyone tell you otherwise!

6. Author's Note: For the record, I was never officially diagnosed with postpartum depression and I fully believe with every ounce of my body I had it.

7. Neff, Kristin. "The Three Elements of Self-Compassion." *Self-Compassion*, self-compassion.org/the-three-elements-of-self-compassion-2/#3elements. Accessed 8 June. 2024.

8. Brock, Sophie. "Alternatives to The Perfect Mother Myth." *The Good Enough Mother Podcast*, 24 May 2021, drsophiebrock.com/podcast58.

9. Djossa, Erica. "The Perfect Mother Myth." *MomWell*, 8 June 2024, www.momwell.com/blog/the-perfect-mother-myth.

10. Will, Madeline. "'Brown v. Board' Decimated the Black Educator Pipeline. A Scholar Explains How." *Education Week*, 16 May 2022, www.edweek.org/teaching-learning/brown-v-board-decimated-the-black-educator-pipeline-a-scholar-explains-how/2022/05.

Chapter Six

1. "Reparenting to Heal the Wounded Inner Child." *CPTSD Foundation*, 27 July 2020, cptsdfoundation.org/2020/07/27/reparenting-to-heal-the-wounded-inner-child/.

2. Wong, Harry K., and Rosemary T. Wong. *The First Days of School: How to Be an Effective Teacher.* 4th ed., Harry K. Wong Publications, 2018.

3. Siegel, Daniel J., and Tina Payne Bryson. *The Whole-Brain Child: 12 Revolutionary Strategies to Nurture Your Child's Developing Mind.* Delacorte Press, 2011.Page 33.

4. "The Toolbox Project." *Toolbox Project*, www.toolboxproject.com. Accessed 8 Oct. 2024.

5. Tatum, Beverly Daniel. *Why Are All the Black Kids Sitting Together in the Cafeteria?* Basic Books, 2017.

6. "If You Don't Think You Have Time to Meditate for an Hour, Meditate for Two." *In-House Staff*, www.in-

housestaff.org/dont-time-meditate-hour-761. Accessed 2 Oct. 2024.

7. Freeman, Emily P. *The Next Right Thing: A Simple, Soulful Practice for Making Life Decisions*. Revell, 2019.

8. *Frozen II*. Directed by Chris Buck and Jennifer Lee, Walt Disney Animation Studios, 2019.

Chapter Seven

1. "Black and White Thinking." *Anxiety Coach*, Mayo Clinic, anxietycoach.mayoclinic.org/depression-coach/ depression-treatment-cognitive-restructuring-copy/. Accessed 8 Oct. 2024.

2. *"Personal Growth: Woulda, Coulda, Shoulda."* Psychology Today, 1 May 2012, www.psychologytoday.com/ca/ blog/the-power-prime/201205/personal-growth-woulda-coulda-shoulda. Accessed 18 July. 2024.

3. Harper, Amber. *Burned-In Teacher*. www.burnedinteacher. com. N.d.

4. Howerton, Kristin. *Rage Against the Minivan*. www. rageagainsttheminivan.com. Accessed 1 October 2024.

5. "What Is the Spiritual Bypass?" *Psychology Today*, 22 Feb. 2023, www.psychologytoday.com/ca/blog/heart-medicine-for-a-changing-world/202302/what-is-the-spiritual-bypass. Accessed 15 May 2024.

6. Moss, Jennifer. "Six Causes of Burnout at Work." *Greater Good Science Center*, University of California, Berkeley, 16 Mar. 2022, greatergood.berkeley.edu/article/item/ six_causes_of_burnout_at_work. Accessed 1 Oct. 2024.

7. Withers, Bill. "Lean on Me." *Just As I Am*, Sussex Records, 1972.

Chapter Eight

1. "Gender Pay Gap Facts." *Pew Research Center*, 1 Mar. 2023, www.pewresearch.org/short-reads/2023/03/01/gender-pay-gap-facts/. N.d.

2. Dubin, Minna. *Mom Rage: The Everyday Crisis of Modern Motherhood.* New World Library, 2023.

3. Goldstein, Dana. *The Teacher Wars: A History of America's Most Embattled Profession.* Doubleday, 2014.

4. Brooks, Alfred Shivy. *Alfred's Laundry.* www.alfredslaundry.com. Accessed 8 Oct. 2024.

5. Peck, Devlin. "Teacher Burnout Statistics: The Numbers You Need to Know." *Devlin Peck*, www.devlinpeck.com/content/teacher-burnout-statistics. Accessed 28 April 2024.

6. Goldstein, Dana. i.b.

7. Goldstein, Dana. *The Teacher Wars: A History of America's Most Embattled Profession.* Doubleday, 2014, p. 26.

8. Howerton, Kristin. *Rage Against the Minivan: Learning to Parent Without Perfectionism.* Convergent Books, 2020.

9. Government of Canada. "EI Maternity and Parental Benefits." *Canada.ca*, www.canada.ca/en/services/benefits/ei/ei-maternity-parental.html. Accessed 27 May. 2024.

10. National Partnership for Women and Families. "Key Facts: The Family and Medical Leave Act." *NationalPartnership.org*, Feb. 2023, www.nationalpartnership.org/report/fmla-key-facts/. Accessed 17 Aug. 2024.

11. Livingston, Gretchen, and Deja Thomas. "Of 41 Countries, Only U.S. Lacks Paid Parental Leave." *Pew Research Center*, 16 Dec. 2019, www.pewresearch.org/short-reads/2019/12/16/u-s-lacks-mandated-paid-parental-leave/. Accessed 17 Aug. 2024.

12. Mosqueda, Emily Adler. *Unexpected: A Postpartum Memoir*. Demeter Press, 2023.

13. Siegel, Daniel J., and Tina Payne Bryson. *The Whole-Brain Child: 12 Revolutionary Strategies to Nurture Your Child's Developing Mind*. Delacorte Press, 2011.

Chapter Nine

1. Haley, Eleanor, and Litsa Williams. *What's Your Grief? Lists to Help You Through Any Loss*. Quirk Books, 2022.

2. Gonzalez, Dalia. "The Importance of Mourning Losses Even When They Seem Small." *NPR*, 2 June 2021, https://www.npr.org/2021/06/02/1002446604/the-importance-of-mourning-losses-even-when-they-seem-small.

3. "Gilroy Garlic Festival Mass Shooting." *NBC Bay Area*, https://www.nbcbayarea.com/news/local/gilroy-garlic-festival-mass-shooting/150424/.

4. "Moms Demand Action." *Moms Demand Action*, https://momsdemandaction.org/.

5. Schumann, Taylor S. "When Thoughts and Prayers Are Not Enough." *Taylor S. Schumann*, https://www.taylorschumann.com/.

6. Children's Hospital of Philadelphia, Center for Violence Protection https://violence.chop.edu/domestic-violence-and-child-abuse#.XvIrg2hKgdU

7. Schuman, Taylor S. i.b.

8. Patterson, Kiera. "ALICE: Active Shooter Training and School Safety." *The Trace*, 3 Dec. 2019, https://www.thetrace.org/2019/12/alice-active-shooter-training-school-safety/.

9. Auman, Jenai. "Life is about the journey, not the destination." *Instagram*, 18 Apr. 2023, https://www.instagram.com/jenaiauman/p/CqVa2_UL52o/.

10. Gilbert, Elizabeth. "Your past is just a story. And once you learn how to tell it, you can change the story." *Facebook*, 24 Feb. 2021, https://www.facebook.com/GilbertLiz/photos/a.356148997800555/3234180116664081/?type=3.

11. "Restorative Justice." *Government of Canada*, https://www.justice.gc.ca/eng/cj-jp/rj-jr/index.html.

12. Source Unknown. Viewed on Instagram.

13. Peck, Devlin. I.b.

14. HYNS Team. "47 Practices to Heal a Dysregulated Nervous System." *Heal Your Nervous System*, 17 May 2023, https://healyournervoussystem.com/47-practices-to-heal-a-dysregulated-nervous-system/. Accessed 12 Aug. 2024.

Chapter Ten

1. Dion, Lisa. "Synthetic Play Therapy Institute." *Synthetic Play Therapy Institute*, 2022, https://syntheticplaytherapy.com/.

2. "ACES and Toxic Stress: Frequently Asked Questions." *Harvard University Center on the Developing Child*, https://developingchild.harvard.edu/resources/aces-and-toxic-stress-frequently-asked-questions/.

3. Author's Note: I use quotations around at-risk, because this is a term I no longer use to describe students or schools.

4. Gotye. "Somebody That I Used to Know." *Making Mirrors*, Universal Republic Records, 2011.

5. Shafler, Katherine Morgan. *The Perfectionist's Guide to Losing Control: A Path to Peace and Power*. 2022.

Chapter Eleven

1. Tolle, Eckhart. *The Power of Now: A Guide to Spiritual Enlightenment.* New World Library, 1999.

2. *White Christmas.* Directed by Michael Curtiz, Paramount Pictures, 1954.

3. Brown, Brené. "The Stories We Tell Ourselves." *YouTube*, 25 Nov. 2015, https://www.youtube.com/watch?v=WyK537UA_E8. Accessed 18 Aug. 2024.

4. Nelson, Portia. *There's a Hole in My Sidewalk: The Romance of Self-Discovery.* 1993.

5. *The Luckiest Club.* The Luckiest Club, www.theluckiestclub.com/. Accessed 8 August 2024.

6. Nelson, Portia. "There's a Hole in My Sidewalk." In *There's a Hole in My Sidewalk: The Romance of Self-Discovery*, 1993.

Chapter Twelve

1. Brown, Brené. *Daring Greatly: How the Courage to Be Vulnerable Transforms the Way We Live, Love, Parent, and Lead.* Gotham Books, 2012.

2. Stabile, Suzanne. *The Journey Toward Wholeness: Enneagram Wisdom for Stress, Balance, and Transformation.* InterVarsity Press, 2020.

3. Pedraza, Julie. "A Simple Guide to the Nine Enneagram Personality Types." *Julie Pedraza*, 29 June 2023, www.juliepedraza.com/enneagram-types-discover-yours/#:~:text=ENNEAGRAM%20PERSONALITY%20TYPES%20EXPLAINED,and%20perspectives%20on%20the%20world. Accessed 30 July 2024.

4. Stabile, Suzanne. "The Next Right Thing." *The Next Right Thing*, hosted by Emily P. Freeman, episode 253, 30 Mar. 2021, emilypfreeman.com/podcast/253/. Accessed 8 August 2024.

5. *Beetlejuice*. Directed by Tim Burton, Warner Bros., 1988.

6. Forleo, Marie. "Don't Overcome Your Perfectionism! Why Your High Standards Make You a Star." *Marie Forleo*, hosted by Katherine Morgan Schafler, 16 May 2023, www.marieforleo.com/blog/katherine-morgan-schafler.

7. Shafler, Katherine Morgan. *The Perfectionist's Guide to Losing Control: A Path to Peace and Power.* Penguin Random House, 2023.

8. Bone, Jamina. *Momming With Truth*. Momming With Truth, 2024.

Chapter Thirteen

1. Kelley, Tom, and David Kelley. *Creative Confidence: Unleashing the Creative Potential Within Us All*. Crown Business, 2013.

2. Rae, Amber. *Choose Wonder Over Worry: Move Beyond Fear and Doubt to Unlock Your Full Potential*. Perigee Books, 2018.

3. Bai, Stephanie. "In Defence of Gen Z." *Maclean's*, vol. 136, no. 3, Mar. 2023.

Index of Tools Offered

Affirmations & Mantras to Try On

- *I am peace.*
- *We are all people with fears.*
- *Anytime I've judged another's situation, it's come back tenfold in my life.*
- *I did the best I could with the information I had at the time.*
- *You are stronger than your scariest thoughts.*
- *Each time you walk through this door, you get a fresh start.*
- *Strength exists in places we can't always see.*
- *Breathe in what I can control. Breathe out what I can't.*
- *I wouldn't let grief happen to me, so it came in like the charging bull it is and said, "You will know me."*
- *When I set down what was never mine to carry, I became free.*
- *I know what will happen if I don't change; I don't know what can happen if I do.*
- *May that be possible for me, too.*
- *Things will grow if we take the time to nurture them.*
- *Everything that's ever been has led me to this moment.*

How to Write Your Own "Letter to Future You."

1. Think of what's been causing you doubt and worry lately. For example: *What are you afraid of? Is there a goal you wish to reach, but it feels miles away? In what areas are you struggling right now?*

2. Think of how far into the future you wish your note to be. (I like to pick five years.)

3. Address the letter to yourself and write as if you've achieved those goals and overcame your current challenges.

   - State where you were before. Adding these facts grounds the letter.

   - Acknowledge what had been hard for you (i.e., what you're struggling with right now).

   - Remember, the goal is to quell your current anxieties by writing as if you have achieved what's on your heart.

   - It's OK to take some liberties. You're utilizing your imagination! It's also OK to write that you didn't achieve all of your goals. This helps the letter feel believable.

   - Have fun and see where it takes you!

4. Come back to this practice as often as needed.

A Template to Get You Started

Hey *(Your Name)*,

I can't believe it's been __*(#)*__ years since _____*(I moved... I took that job... etc.)*_____. I was so worried about never being _____ , yet, here I am. It's been challenging, but I'm so happy to write that _____*(the goal you achieved)*_____.

Space For You
Use as Needed

_____

_____

_____

_____

_____

_____

_____

_____

_____

_____

_____

_____

_____

_____

_____

_____

www.ingramcontent.com/pod-product-compliance
Lightning Source LLC
Chambersburg PA
CBHW021216130626
46554CB00004B/1249